THE UNIVERSITY I

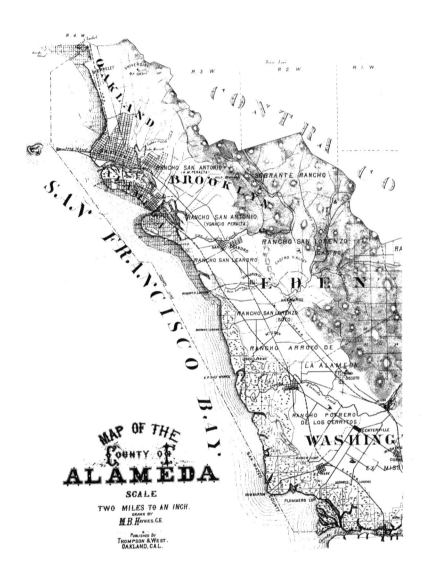

The County of Alameda in 1878. The University is in the foothills at the extreme north.

THE UNIVERSITY IN THE 1870s

William Hammond Hall and the
Original Campus Plan
by Kent Watson

The University and the
Constitutional Convention of 1878
by Peter S. Van Houten

Chapters in the History of the
University of California
Number Six

Center for the Studies in Higher Education and
Institute of Governmental Studies
University of California, Berkeley
1996

Library of Congress Cataloging-In-Publication Data

The university in the 1870s.
      p. cm. — (Chapters in the history of the University of California ; no. 6)
   Includes bibliographical references.
   Contents: William Hammond Hall and the original campus plan / by Kent Watson—The university and the constitutional convention of 1878 / by Peter Van Houten.
   ISBN 0-87772-370-2
   1. University of California (1868-1952)—Buildings—History—19th century. 2. University of California, Berkeley—Buildings—History—19th century. 3. University of California, Berkeley--Charters. 4. Agricultural colleges—United States—History—19th century. 5. Hall, Wm. Ham. (William Hammond) I. Watson, Kent. II. Van Houten, Peter. III. Series.
LD759.U55 1996
378.794'67—dc20   96-8769
                                                                CIP

In honor of the 125th anniversary of the founding of the University of California, the Center for Studies in Higher Education at Berkeley, in cooperation with the Institute of Governmental Studies, takes pleasure in publishing a series of "chapters" in the history of the University. These are designed to illuminate particular problems and periods in the history of U.C., especially its oldest and original campus at Berkeley, and to identify special turning points or features in the "long century" of the University's evolution. Histories are stories meant to be read and enjoyed in their own right, but the editors cannot conceal the hope that readers of these chapters will notice facts and ideas pertinent to the decade that closes our own century and millennium.

Carroll Brentano and
Sheldon Rothblatt, editors

Carroll W. Brentano is an architectural historian and Project Coordinator of the University History Project, Center for Studies in Higher Education at the University of California, Berkeley. Sheldon Rothblatt is Professor Emeritus of History and former director of the Center for Studies in Higher Education, University of California, Berkeley.

Figure 1: Ezra Slocum Carr, professor of agriculture, 1869-1874, and regent, 1875-1880.

CONTENTS

FOREWORD

These two essays, one about a plan for the University's physical campus, the other about the University's change of constitutional status, have, at first glance, only a chronological connection—they deal with events taking place within the same five years, 1873 to 1878. Therefore, a few words of introduction are needed to assure the reader that the two essays are not so far apart in subject matter. In fact, in both plot and cast of characters the two dramas have much the same focus. That focus, broadly speaking, is the era of the arrival of the discipline of agriculture into American higher education.

Two landmarks of this agricultural era, which stretches from 1868 to 1910,[1] remain today on the Berkeley campus. One is the University's first building, the College of Agriculture (South Hall) of 1873, and the other is the large open grassy space in the northwest corner of the campus—the original hayfield. Looking at the William Hammond Hall plan for the campus of 1873 (Figure 6) with its gardens, fields, orchards, and the farmhouse of the professor of agriculture of which Kent Watson tells us,[2] the Berkeley picture much resembles the campuses of other state agricultural colleges. Iowa's,[3] 1864, the Amherst campus of the University of Massachusetts, designed by Frederick Law Olmsted, 1866, Maine State's (also by Olmsted), 1867, Michigan State's and Kansas State's, both the 1870s[4] are called by the historian of the American campus, Paul Turner, "The Democratic College." He quotes planner Olmsted's ideas on the subject, as

---

[1] The beginning of this era is discussed below, the end came with the removal of the University Farm to Davis in 1909, coupled with the ending of the Agricultural Experiment Stations across California. The recently published *Science and Service, A History of the Land-Grant University and Agriculture in California*, by Ann Foley Scheuring (Oakland, Calif., 1995), covers this period in full and fascinating detail.

[2] Another memory of the agricultural era is the replacement of that farmhouse by the President's House, begun in 1900, finished, and presented to the president in 1911, at the end of the era, as it were.

[3] Earle D. Ross, *The Land-Grant Idea at Iowa State College* (Ames, Iowa, 1958), figure p. 75. The founders of Iowa State attended a meeting at the Sheffield School where Daniel Coit Gilman heard Senator Morrill speak about the true intention of his Land Grant Bill, p. 41, (see Van Houten, p. 69).

[4] These plans of agricultural colleges and comments about them are found in Paul Turner, *Campus: An American Planning Tradition* (Cambridge, Mass., 1984), 140-53.

expressed in his 1866 pamphlet *A Few Things to be Thought of Before Proceeding to Plan Buildings for the National Agricultural Colleges.* Olmsted opposed the view of South Carolina's Chancellor Harper who assumed that "even the elementary instruction of a common school would not only be wasted, but would be positively detrimental to the interests of society at large, if given to men who were afterwards to be employed in occupations in which manual labor was an important element." Olmsted took instead the position of Massachusetts's Abbott Lawrence that, in New England, the working farmer or mechanic not only "reads similar books, wears similar clothing, . . . dwells in a similar house, with similar furniture, to that of members of professions or trades whose labor . . . [is] of a widely different character from his," but also "a law constituting an institution for the education of farmers, with a generic title relating it to a class of educational institutions in which hitherto men have been fitted almost exclusively for quite different callings, evidently proceeds from an impulse of the same general current of conviction."[5] In other words, the education, like the furniture, of farmers, is, in the northern states, held to be the same as that of young men of the leisure classes.

The law referred to by Olmsted as establishing this view, is one the reader will encounter many times in these two essays: it is the Land Grant Act passed by Congress in 1862, commonly called after its author, the Morrill Act. Although Senator Justin Morrill claimed that his legislation was wrongly titled an "Agricultural College Act" (a clerk had made an error in the superscription), so it came to be called, and that title was thought by a great many people to rightly express its intent, as you will read in these essays. The Morrill Act provided that the proceeds from the sale of land given by the federal government to each state, was to be for the

> endowment, support and maintenance of at least one college where the leading object shall be, without excluding other scientific and classical studies, and including military tactics, to teach such branches of learning as are related to agriculture and mechanical arts, in such manner as the legislatures of the States may respectively prescribe, in order to promote the liberal and practical

---

[5]Frederick Law Olmsted, *A Few Things to be Thought of before Proceeding to Plan Buildings for the National Agricultural Colleges* (New York, 1866), 10.

education of the industrial classes in the several pursuits and professions of life.[6]

Today, we can easily see where the trouble lay: reading "the leading object shall be . . . to teach such branches of learning as are related to agriculture and mechanical arts," gives one impression, reading the part omitted from the preceding "without excluding other scientific and classical studies" gives quite another. Each side took up one of these as an interpretation of the meaning of the act, and used that reading to bolster their demands for precedence, or at least equality, in the allocation of buildings and faculty resources.

In 1873 William Hammond Hall assumed that he had to fight off the professor of agriculture to properly design the campus, and in 1878 the University's regents thought that the very existence of their institution was under the threat of demolition by the agriculturists of the state.

Interestingly, the same man turns out to be the chief villain in both Watson's and Van Houten's stories. If ever a university professor were to have earned the name "controversial" it was California's first professor of agriculture, Ezra Carr. Carr, born in 1819 in upstate New York, graduated from Rensselaer Polytechnic Institute (model for the engineering colleges just emerging), and, with a later M.D. degree, landed at the University of Wisconsin in 1856 teaching agricultural chemistry and natural history. The story of Carr's turbulent career at Wisconsin is remarkably similar to his six years, 1869 to 1875, at California. Eccentric as a teacher, embroiled in political feuds, disputatious with colleagues and administrators, finally accused of minor theft, he left Wisconsin in 1867 affronted, but he "sweetly offered the regents his 'active sympathies and cooperation.'"[7]

In these essays you will read how the California Ezra Carr took the part of the Grangers against the University's regents, demanded special arrangements for the agricultural program on the campus and, to planner Hall's annoyance, put his two cents into the grading of the grounds. When he was fired by President Gilman, the reason given was incompetence—lack of scientific distinction, easy classes, nonattendance at faculty meetings. Carr's side of it was his enthusiastic personal involvement with the farmers: lecturing, demonstrating, becoming a Grange official himself, repeatedly

---

[6]Ross, *Land-Grant Idea*, 5.

[7]Merle Curti and Vernon Carstensen, *The University of Wisconsin: A History, 1848-1925*, Vol. 1 (Madison, Wis., 1949), 180-81.

petitioning the legislature for funds for the furtherance of agricultural education at the University and the regents for plants and workmen to put in the practical crops on the campus.[8]

Readers of our two essays here will not be surprised, having this thumbnail sketch of the biggest troublemaker of the 1870s, to learn that, according to Carr's enemies, it was his wife Jeanne who put him up to much of his mischief, wrote his letters, and masterminded his politics. But it may startle them to learn that California's greatest hero of the same era, John Muir, spoke of Mrs. Carr as "dear, dear, spiritual mother" and of her letters "How good and wise they seem to be!"[9] Of Carr himself, Muir said "[he] first laid before me the great book of Nature," and Ralph Waldo Emerson owed the beginning of his friendship with Muir to the Carrs.[10] Mrs. Carr also appears as heroine in another of our "Chapters": Geraldine Clifford in *Equally in View* says that Josephine Corella, member of the first UC class to admit women, in later years told an interviewer that it was through the intervention of Jeanne Carr that "we girls were allowed to enter the University."[11]

Another, much less painful, disagreement sketched out by Kent Watson, is that between William Hammond Hall, and his, what today would be called, mentor, Frederick Law Olmsted. Their correspondence, some of which is published here for the first time, introduces us to an Olmsted who, while graciously sending helpful suggestions to Hall, did not like to have his pronouncements challenged: he takes Hall to task for planning too much lawn, chides him for being insufficiently humble, and expects Hall to carry these complaints to President Gilman.

One more name to conjure with: Daniel Coit Gilman, a hero in both essays. He came to the California presidency in 1874 from Yale's Sheffield engineering school, intended to create a modern and useful university, suffered like Hall under the scourge of the representatives of agriculture, and took the pleasant way out in 1876 by accepting an invitation to be the founding president of Johns Hopkins. Meanwhile, a California friend and admirer of Gilman, the John Dwinelle who had been the staunch friend of

---

[8]For Ezra Carr's life see Scheuring, *Science and Service*, 11-22.

[9]William Badé, *Life and Letters of John Muir* (Boston, 1923), I, 383, 26.

[10]*Ibid.,* I, 143, 258.

[11]Geraldine Clifford, *"Equally in View",* the University of California, Its Women, and the Schools (Berkeley, 1995), 20.

Figure 2: Daniel Coit Gilman, president of the University, 1872-1875.

the University and of its parent, the College of California, and who had sacrificed himself to public scorn to protect the honor of the regents wrote the following bittersweet letter to the departing president:

> We have not provided you with the entertainment to which you were invited. We are on the eve of a contest where the Board of Regents is to be assailed by falsehood, malice and every kind of nastiness from the outside, aided by treachery from within. We did not invite you to this, and you have a right to retire from it, particularly when the mode of retirement comes in the accepted reward for well-doing—promotion.[12]

But, as Van Houten tells us, Gilman's advice and encouragement were later offered from Baltimore and used by the beleaguered regents in 1878-79.

All in all, this was an adventurous, not to say traumatic, decade for the infant University. In the long story not much happened, and the same adventures were being lived through by dozens of other new American universities—this was the era of the birth of the A and M college. But to Hall and Gilman in 1874, and to the "friends of the University" in 1878, the threats were real and the University of California has no reason to be ashamed of the 1870s.

Carroll Brentano

---

[12]Fabian Franklin, *The Life of Daniel Coit Gilman* (New York, 1910), 172.

ILLUSTRATIONS

WILLIAM HAMMOND HALL AND THE ORIGINAL CAMPUS PLAN

by Kent Watson

ACKNOWLEDGMENTS & DEDICATION

Since this article is an outgrowth of my 1989 master's thesis, "A Forgotten Chapter in the History of Landscape Architecture: William Hammond Hall and the 1873 University of California, Berkeley Plan," I am indebted to those who started me on this intriguing path of historical research: Russell Beatty, retired, and Michael Laurie, of the UC Berkeley Department of Landscape Architecture, who first suggested the topic, and thesis committee members Michael Southworth and Jim Leiby.

Mary Ellen Jones, then manuscript librarian and guardian of Hall's papers at the Bancroft Library, was especially helpful in assisting and supporting my research efforts. Others who deserve recognition include: Bill Roberts, the University Archivist, and Professor Gunther Barth, History Department. Professor Barth was largely instrumental in getting me involved with the University History Seminar, organized by the Center for Studies in Higher Education, which became the birthplace for this article. As one of the few off-campus and nonacademic types attending these gatherings, I appreciated the opportunity to be part of this scholarly group as it explored the various aspects of University history.

I am especially grateful for the assistance and continuing support of two individuals: my wife Margaret, who knows well the rigors of academic research, and Carroll Brentano, the University History Project Coordinator, through whose good humor, editing, and cajoling I managed to produce this article.

Figure 3: William Hammond Hall, circa 1873.

THE ORIGINAL 1873 BERKELEY CAMPUS PLAN
OF WILLIAM HAMMOND HALL

by Kent E. Watson

When the University of California was founded in March 1868, there was no Berkeley campus, only an undeveloped site north of Oakland owned by the College of California, a private institution that opened its doors in Oakland in 1860. As part of the arrangement creating the University as the land grant school, the College of California merged with the new institution and ceded its Berkeley site to the University. In 1869 the new Board of Regents promptly requested a campus plan for the Berkeley site.[1] In the following year construction began on South Hall, the first permanent building, but lack of funds delayed completion for three years.[2]

Ultimately, however, the plan that guided the development of the grounds of the new university campus during its first quarter century, *Proposed Plan for the Improvement of the Site of the University of California at Berkeley*, was prepared in 1873 by William Hammond Hall, a young engineer and landscape architect. (Figure 3)

Hall, a largely self-taught engineer, made in his lifetime two significant contributions to landscape architecture: the original design for Golden Gate Park in San Francisco (1871) and the Berkeley campus plan (1873). He developed these plans with the advice and counsel (through correspondence) of Frederick Law Olmsted, the founder of the profession of landscape architecture. Although Olmsted has, at times, been erroneously credited with both of these plans, in recent years several publications have recognized Hall's formerly unsung involvement in the creation of Golden Gate Park. However, although many aspects of Hall's campus plan were implemented in the 25 years after its creation, almost nothing has been published about his work in Berkeley. Only in the 1988 publication of

---

[1]Katherine Williams Bolton, "The History of Landscape Design on the University of California, Berkeley Campus," masters thesis (Berkeley, 1981), 13. Hereafter: Bolton, "History."

[2]William Warren Ferrier, *The Origin and Development of the University of California* (Berkeley, 1930), 319-20, 349-50. Hereafter: Ferrier, *Origin*.

Michael Laurie's history of the Department of Landscape Architecture at Berkeley is Hall mentioned.[3]

Hall went on to become the first state engineer and to make a large contribution in the field of water use in California. In the profession of landscape architecture Hall's contributions were thought noteworthy enough by Olmsted to recommend him for a committee of American landscape architects to review the landscape integrity of the grounds in the nation's capital that Olmsted had proposed in 1874.[4]

WILLIAM HAMMOND HALL:
EDUCATION AND EARLY CAREER

William Hammond Hall was born in Hagerstown, Maryland, on February 12, 1846 to Anna Maria (Hammond) and John Buchanan Hall. The family came to California in 1850, eventually settling in Stockton in 1853. Young William, an only son, attended a private Stockton academy from 1858 to 1865, under the tutelage of an Episcopal clergyman. He gained a practical education as a civil engineer when he worked on survey crews for the U.S. Engineer Corps in Oregon and California, from 1863 to 1865, meanwhile studying under a now unknown private tutor.

Although the family had wanted him to attend West Point, the outbreak of the Civil War led his southern mother to rule against that choice, and consequently he never attended college. Since he had prepared for West Point, however, he was well versed in mathematics.[5]

---

[3]Michael Laurie, *75 Years of Landscape Architecture at Berkeley, Part 1* (Berkeley, 1988), 2.

[4]Frederick Law Olmsted to William Hammond Hall, March 28, 1874, William Hammond Hall papers, Bancroft Library, University of California, Berkeley, (hereafter: FLO to WHH, date), 3-4. This is part of the collection of Hall's papers that includes 26 original handwritten letters from Olmsted to Hall. The author is indebted to Mary Ellen Jones, then the manuscript librarian at the Bancroft Library, for her assistance and ardent support of this endeavor.

[5]Mary Ellen Jones, "William Hammond Hall: An Engineer with Vision," in *Bancroftiana* 96 (Berkeley, 1988), 10-12. (Hereafter: Jones, "Hall.") Los Angeles Examiner (pub), "Notables of the Southwest," in *Press Reference Library* (Los Angeles, 1912), 121. (Hereafter: Examiner, *Library*.) Raymond H. Clary in his book, *The Making of Golden Gate Park - The Early Years: 1865-1906* (San Francisco, 1984), 7-8 (hereafter: Clary, *Making*), and in a personal interview on

From 1865 to 1871 Hall spent most of his time on the highly detailed topographic mapping of the entire San Francisco peninsula, using a plane table in the field. He also made surveys from San Diego to Neah Bay, Washington. In 1870, having married Emma Kate Fitzhugh, from a distinguished southern family, he settled in San Francisco. They had three daughters.[6]

During this period Hall was apparently able to gain some insights on the principles of landscape design through travels to Europe and the eastern United States. According to a 1871 letter to Frederick Law Olmsted, he "visited and carefully studied and noted the principal parks and grounds about London, Paris and in the United States; particularly have I roamed through your Central Park and the Fairmount and the Brooklyn and the Druid Hill...."[7]

While Hall was launching his career as a civil engineer, interested San Francisco citizens were asking Frederick Law Olmsted to prepare a report on a park. In 1866 Olmsted recommended a major park for the city, but not a traditional one with trees and shrubs: "It would not be wise nor safe to undertake to form a park upon any plan which assumed as a certainty that trees which delight the eye can be made to grow near San Francisco." As the park site he chose Hayes Valley, the area west of the modern Civic Center which included major connections to, and enhancement of, Market Street and Van Ness Avenue. Deemed too expensive, the plan was rejected by the

---

April 18, 1989, Mr. Clary provided some additional color on Hall's upbringing, largely based upon a speech that Hall gave to the American Society of Civil Engineers in 1929. Clary hand-typed a copy of most of the speech for use in his book and made it available to the author: it is cited as Hall, "Recollections of Early California Engineering" (San Francisco, 1929), 2 (hereafter: Hall, "Recollections"). Unfortunately, Clary was unable to recall who had had the original manuscript of the speech. Ray Clary, a friend and longtime supporter of Hall and Golden Gate Park, died in January 1992 at age 75.

[6]Hall, "Recollections," 2, 7-8. Examiner, *Library*, 121.

[7]William Hammond Hall to Frederick Law Olmsted, August 22, 1871, Frederick Law Olmsted Papers, Manuscript Division, Library of Congress, Washington, D.C., 3 (hereafter: FLO Papers). This is the only known copy of this pivotal letter, in which the unknown Hall, rather presumptuously, introduces himself to Olmsted, the well-known landscape architect, and requests his advice and counsel on the design of Golden Gate Park.

city.[8] Ironically, had Olmsted's plan been implemented the depressed boulevard design for Van Ness Avenue might have saved a number of structures along that street which had to be dynamited to stop the spread of flames in the 1906 earthquake and fire. Nevertheless, public interest in a major city park continued. After the title was settled to the Outside Lands, in the western half of the city, a group of prominent citizens lobbied for a large park there. In April 1870, four years after Olmsted's plan had been rejected, the state passed a law designating that site as "Golden Gate Park" and creating a commission for its control and management.[9]

Hall's previous work on the San Francisco peninsula had included topographic mapping of the Outside Lands. Therefore, it was logical that in August 1870 he was awarded the contract by the San Francisco Park Commissioners for the topographic survey of the new park. His report, maps, and plans for the early work on the park were adopted by the commission on February 15, 1871, and in August of that year he was appointed engineer and superintendent of Golden Gate Park. He was 25 years old. Hall remained superintendent for five years until he resigned in 1876, after which he continued to serve without compensation as consulting engineer for many years. On Hall's recommendation, in 1887 the commission hired John McLaren, a Scottish gardener and landscape designer, as park superintendent. McLaren, due largely to his strong will, flamboyant style, and longevity—he served until he died at age 97—continues to receive credit for much of the work that originated with Hall for the development of the park.[10]

Hall had learned various methods of sand dune reclamation from his experience with the army engineers under General Barton S. Alexander. During the topographic survey of Golden Gate Park, a fortunate accident involving some spilled barley led him to devise a method for stabilizing the

---

[8]Laura Wood Roper, *FLO: A Biography of Frederick Law Olmsted*, (Baltimore, 1973), 304. (Hereafter: Roper, *FLO*.)

[9]Clary, *Making*, 11.

[10]San Francisco Park Commissioners, "First Biennial Report of the San Francisco Park Commissioners, 1870-71" (San Francisco, 1872), 6-7. (Hereafter: Commissioners, "Report.") Clary, *Making*, 7, 76-77. Jones, "Hall," 11. (Editor's note: In an earlier "Chapter in the History of the University of California" (number two, 1994), *California's Practical Period*, Gunther Barth has told the story of the creation of Golden Gate Park in some detail.)

drifting sands that occupied most of the western half of the thousand-acre park site. By mixing the fast-growing barley with slower-growing lupine seeds, he found the barley would shelter the lupine until it was established, thus securing the sands for small trees.[11]

The barley experiment served Hall well in stabilizing the site, but how this self-trained engineer-surveyor developed the understanding and skills to become a landscape designer, without any formal training, is a matter for speculation. A speech that Hall made in his eighties, as an elder of engineering in California, may provide some insight. He "was by nature an out-of-door boy, communing with nature on every fitting occasion; and learning some fundamental facts of nature's worked (sic) or had worked them out. I was a thoughtful observer. . . ." He goes on,

> my mind was specially opened to the graphic method. Anything
> that could be clearly shown by a draft, a picture, or a model made
> a good and lasting impression. Obviously, geometry, most parts of
> physics and most natural sciences, were easy to me. At certain
> stages of my progress I devoured every book that came into my
> way, relating to them.[12]

Meanwhile, Hall's plans for "grading the Avenue [through the present-day Panhandle] from Baker to Stanyan streets"[13] were adopted by the Park Commission in February 1871. More detailed plans for the layout of park facilities and landscape improvements in the eastern end of the park came later that year, after Hall had begun his correspondence with Frederick Law Olmsted.

HALL AND OLMSTED:
THE BEGINNING OF A LONG RELATIONSHIP

Hall, during these formative years of his career, was undoubtedly aware of Olmsted's work, both in the East with Central Park and in the West with his plans for Oakland's Mountain View Cemetery (1864), a report for Yosemite Park in 1865, the 1866 park proposal for San Francisco, and in the

---

[11]Clary, *Making*, 14-15. William Hammond Hall, "The Romance of a Woodland Park - Golden Gate Park, 1870-1890," unpublished manuscript (San Francisco, c. 1926), 206. (Hereafter: Hall, "Romance.")

[12]Hall, "Recollections," 2.

[13]Clary, *Making*, 13.

same year the College of California plan in Berkeley.[14] Having completed the topographic survey for the park, Hall now faced the challenge of preparing a development plan, and so, as soon as he was appointed superintendent, he boldly took the initiative and wrote to Olmsted, whom he had never met, for advice.[15] In this letter, of August 22, 1871, Hall requested his suggestions on the "pleasure grounds for San Francisco." Olmsted's response, on October 5, 1871, delayed by a month's absence from his office, repeats from his 1866 report that it may not be practicable to develop a traditional park in San Francisco for "unreflecting people bred in the Atlantic states and the North of Europe." He then notes that "the conditions are so peculiar and the difficulties so great that I regard the problem as unique and that it must be solved if at all by wholly new means & methods. It requires instruction, not adaptation."[16]

In his letter to Olmsted, Hall had asked for a "list of works on Land-scape Architecture." Olmsted provided 13 references on horticulture and on estate and garden design. From a cursory review of these books today, it is easy to see that Hall, with his thirst for knowledge, graphic orientation, and understanding of natural systems and topography, could have readily absorbed enough information to draw a credible plan, not only, as it turned out, for Golden Gate Park, but also for another Olmsted project, the campus in Berkeley.

THE COLLEGE OF CALIFORNIA AND THE UNIVERSITY OF CALIFORNIA: THE HISTORICAL CONTEXT AND OLMSTED'S ROLE

The site of the University of California, Berkeley, campus was first acquired by the College of California in 1858. The College was a private institution chartered in 1855 by a group of men who sought to provide California with the educational status enjoyed by their eastern counterparts. The site, chosen by the College's trustees and the president, Henry Durant, after a long search, was formally dedicated by the trustees in a ceremony held on April 16, 1860 at Founders' Rock. Later that year the College of

---

[14]Roper, *FLO*, 277, 283-87, 303-05, 305-09.

[15]WHH to FLO, August 22, 1871, Hall papers, Library of Congress.

[16]FLO to WHH, October 5, 1871, Hall papers, Bancroft Library.

California formally opened its doors to students in its original downtown Oakland quarters.[17]

In 1864 the College trustees asked Frederick Law Olmsted, who was then managing the Mariposa Company mining operations at Bear Valley in the Sierra Nevada foothills, to develop plans for their new Berkeley site.[18] He worked on the Berkeley project during 1865, presenting the college trustees with his completed plan and 26-page report on June 29, 1866.[19]

Originally, Olmsted had thought of the college grounds as a park, writing in early 1865 that he intended to lay out the college "on the Llewellyn plan," a reference to A. J. Davis's 1850s park-like design for a suburban town in New Jersey.[20] As described by Olmsted in his completed report, when he first visited the site "it was proposed that the buildings . . . should be placed upon a site which looked down upon the surrounding country on every side except that which would be to their rear, and that the remainder of the property should be formed into a *Park*."[21] On further study, however, he determined that such a solution would be both inappropriate and inconvenient and "would permanently entail burdensome expenses upon your institution." Instead, he devised a plan for the small college and its immediate campus setting. The remainder of the land would be devoted to a residential neighborhood.[22]

Drawing upon the picturesque concepts he had used in his Central Park plan, Olmsted aligned a central axis with the spectacular Golden Gate. Then, using the natural land forms to site the few proposed roads and buildings, he created a large park surrounded by park-like residential areas. Even though Olmsted proposed a system of hydrant irrigation, he still tried to dissuade the college trustees from using turf—it would be better to respect the dry Mediterranean climate of the region.[23]

---

[17]Ferrier, *Origin*, 143, 184, 181, 212, 214.

[18]Roper, *FLO*, 305-09.

[19]Frederick Law Olmsted, *Report upon a Projected Improvement of the Estate of the College of California at Berkeley, near Oakland* (San Francisco, 1866). (Hereafter: FLO, *Report*.)

[20]Roper, *FLO*, 277.

[21]FLO, *Report*, 3.

[22]*Ibid.*, 3-5.

[23]*Ibid.*, 22-23.

11

Since Olmsted's original plan has been lost—a curious loss since it was "a very large map some nine feet by five"[24]—we have only the small reduced plan and the report for reference. On the whole, his plan was more general and schematic than that later produced by Hall, as Olmsted was more concerned with the general context of the campus in its environs. For example, he indicated the site for only two college buildings (at the head of the axis): one a library and its collections, the other a general assembly hall and classrooms.[25] Hall's plan for the state university eight years later went into considerable detail in the siting and specific uses of the various university buildings.[26]

Two years after Olmsted had submitted his campus plan to the trustees of the College of California, and before any construction had begun on the Berkeley site, the governor signed into law the Organic Act of March 23, 1868, that created a new institution, the University of California. As part of the arrangement, the College of California merged with it and ceded its Berkeley site to the new university. The new Board of Regents then commissioned new plans for the campus from the architectural firm of Wright and Sanders in the summer of 1869. After a disagreement with the regents over the amount they were to be paid for its services, the firm withdrew its plans from consideration.[27] But the University archives contains the firm's 14-page report, dated July 6, 1869, and one perspective drawing labeled "General View of University Buildings."[28] This plan has three large buildings arranged in a very formal, classical manner, and in no

---

[24]Samuel H. Willey, *A History of the College of California* (San Francisco, 1887), 209.

[25]FLO, *Report*, 24-26.

[26]William Hammond Hall, *Proposed Plan for the Improvement of the Site of the University of California, designed at the request of the Board of Regents by William Hammond Hall, C.E., 1873*, plan map (San Francisco, 1873). Hereafter: Hall, *Proposed Plan*. The plan graphically depicts and, in an extensive note, describes the specific sites and their uses.

[27]Bolton, "History," 13.

[28]Wright and Sanders, Letter to Board of Regents, July 6, 1869 (Berkeley, 1869), in the University of California Archives, Box 1, Folder 14; and "General View of University Buildings," facsimile of perspective drawing, University Archives, (Berkeley, c. 1870).

way resembles the campus that evolved over the next 25 years.[29] Nor does the second plan adopted by the regents in August 1869 when they selected another architectural firm, Kenitzer and Farquharson, to put up the first two buildings, finished in 1873, on the Berkeley site, one for agriculture and the other "academic." Meanwhile, a caretaker was hired and the planting of trees begun.[30]

THE UNIVERSITY OF CALIFORNIA CAMPUS PLAN: HALL'S FIRST CONTACT AND PROPOSAL

How Hall came to devise a plan for the new University of California at Berkeley is not known. We can imagine that as a young and relatively unknown engineer trying to establish a professional practice, he examined a variety of options. Meanwhile, the events revolving around the new university were well covered by the local press,[31] and the fact that California was to have its own reputable institution for research and higher learning that would give it the stature to compete with the East Coast must have been exciting to contemplate. Hall's successes with the Golden Gate Park project during his first two years as engineer and superintendent, probably encouraged him to seek other large tracts to plan—among which would be the University grounds.

The inaugural speech of Daniel Coit Gilman, a noted professor from Yale, and second president of the University, on November 7, 1872, was widely reported. Its theme was "The Building of the University," and in it Gilman praised the considerable wonders and resources of "this new empire State. California, queen of the Pacific. . . ." The president emphasized that two specific goals of his new institution, as specified in the charter, were represented in its very name: first, that it was a university, the most comprehensive of educational institutions, not a college or industrial school. Second, it was "the University of this State," which must be representative

---

[29]The lack of recognition noted earlier for Hall's plan may be due, in part, to a filing error in the University Archives. Unfortunately, a preliminary version of Hall's campus plan in the Bancroft Library with an incomplete tital block and no further identification was incorrectly attributed to Wright and Sanders. As the result of this author's research this error has since been corrected.

[30]Bolton, "History," 14.

[31]Ferrier, *Origin*, 335-42.

of its people and "their undeveloped resources." Gilman urged his audience to look ahead and build on the state's achievements in science and technology. Similarly, paying tribute to the work of the army engineers, he identified the need for civil, mining, and mechanical engineers.[32]

As a relatively new engineer himself, Hall must have felt a kinship with Gilman's call for action. Two months later, perhaps Hall was in the audience when President Gilman gave a speech on "Technical Education" at the Mechanics' Institute in San Francisco.[33] Whatever the circumstances, we know that Hall wrote a note on April 8, 1873, to Samuel F. Butterworth, a regent of the University, offering his services "without fee" and asking to whom he should address his proposal.[34] It may be that Hall chose this recipient because Butterworth was one of the commissioners of Golden Gate Park where Hall was employed. Butterworth passed the note on to President Gilman, who, on April 19, 1873, wrote to Hall on behalf of the regents accepting his "generous offer."[35] While Hall's offer was generous, it was not entirely altruistic. By donating only his own time, he would get his name in front of a body of leading businessmen of the new state and develop some additional business as a result. Of course, he did charge for expenses and for the salaries of those who assisted him.

Hall's detailed proposal for the project followed a week later, on April 28, 1873. In a five-page letter to Gilman, he laid out in considerable detail his ideas.[36] Since this is our first look at Hall's own plans for the campus, it may be helpful to quote from his letter—penned in bold flowing strokes.

After an introductory paragraph, Hall immediately states the need for a plan: "Unfortunately there is not that appreciation of the importance of a prearranged and definite plan for such works, which there should be." He then gives his views regarding the grounds around public buildings, noting that some regard them as unimportant accessories to the main architectural

[32]*Ibid.*, 337.

[33]*Ibid.*, 341.

[34]Hall to S. F. Butterworth, April 8, 1873 (University Archives, Box 1, Folder 15).

[35]Daniel Coit Gilman letter to Hall, April 19, 1873 (Hall papers, Bancroft Library).

[36]Hall to Gilman, April 28, 1873 (Hall papers, Bancroft Library).

Figure 4: The University campus in 1873 looking west, the College of Agriculture (South Hall) on the left, and the College of Letters (North Hall) on the right. (Note the curved road in foreground.)

features, and not as settings to the gem, which they really are, essential parts of an harmonious whole, suggestive of its character, in keeping with the design, and promotive of its convenient and effective use.

Then Hall, to emphasize his case, quotes directly from Sir Humphrey Repton's *The Art of Landscape Gardening* (shown with italics):

All rational improvement of grounds is necessarily founded on a due attention to the character of the Institution of which they form a part, a thorough study of the situation to be handled, and of the climatic and neighborhood influences to which it is subjected.

We see further evidence of his readings in landscape design when he points out that though "the situation [site] is of course a natural formation," it must "be adapted by Art to the uses required," so, while elaborating on the needs of the institution, its natural site, climate, and neighborhood, Hall again emphasizes the importance of aesthetic considerations:

All such improvements, however blessed by nature their site may be, must be regarded, from their inception, as works of art. Nature does not provide lands shaped and drained and planted to suit specific purposes. We are to seize her salient features, and allot them to our definite requirements, and while preserving her more attractive spots in their integrity, develop an intricacy, a diversity of details; presenting a succession of pleasing situations, varied in character, yet so arranged as to be in accordance with each other.

The young engineer gratuitously admonishes his client for the lack of a prior plan: "It is to be regretted that a settled plan of operations for the improvement of the University site has not been adopted before," and even a plan "based upon superficial study, is preferable to a piecemeal and indefinite mode."

Hall's insight into the critical relationship between the educational institution and its grounds emerges in one short paragraph:

The arrangement of these grounds constitutes something more than the laying out of Avenues and the planting of trees. It is, in reality, the planning of the material University. Neither one nor all of the buildings which are to be placed there make up this institution in its entirety.

He speaks of the site as being "one large structure in which the several buildings, designed as they will be for different purposes, are as rooms or wings allotted to such specific uses. . . ." But, while the buildings are "superior in importance, and requiring a greater share of study," they are no more distinctive "than the Botanic garden . . . the departments for the illustration of practical Horticulture, and experimental Agriculture, or even the recreation grounds, the ramble in the woods, or the mere landscape effects."

While the existing buildings must be respected, the proposed buildings, their uses, their proper sites should be related, and the decisions regarding the "architectural structures which are to be erected" should come before "planning for the improvement of the grounds" and the general tone of the site be determined—whether "architectural or natural."

Again, we see evidence of Hall's sensitivity to the landscape:

I suggest that a natural style for the landscape effects be adopted as far as consistent with a proper gradation from the building into the body of the grounds, only heightened in effect by such slight architectural works as are absolutely necessary for convenience and contrast.

In conclusion, although he has some ideas for "the apportioning of the grounds," it is up to the "gentlemen" (the regents) of the University

to state distinctly what are your requirements in this respect—what are the principal features you desire to be embraced in a plan for improvement. I will then endeavor to locate these properly, and fill in details, so as to render their use convenient and pleasurable.

Unfortunately, no record of Gilman's response to Hall has been found.

PREPARATION OF THE PRELIMINARY PLAN

While continuing to work on Golden Gate Park, during the next two months Hall completed a preliminary version of his campus plan and prepared a lengthy letter of transmittal to Gilman discussing its features. This is dated June 2.[37] Although we can only speculate as to existing conditions at the Berkeley site when Hall began his plan, we know that "the main architectural structures" (North and South Halls) were already in place and would be respected.[38] Some roads, particularly along Strawberry Creek, had been built and trees, perhaps as many as 3,400, planted.[39] Hall, however,

---

[37]Hall to Gilman, June 2, 1873 (Hall papers, Bancroft Library).
[38]Hall to Gilman, April 28, 1873 (Hall papers, Bancroft Library).
[39]Bolton, "History," 14.

was displeased with their placement.[40] An 1873 photographic view shows a roughly curvilinear road as an extension of the present-day College Avenue (Figure 4).[41] This road appears in Hall's plan and may have existed when he began his work. Unfortunately, the topographic base map that Hall used has not been found.

That Hall thoughtfully considered his pivotal role in the future of the University is apparent in his June 2nd letter to Gilman transmitting "the scheme for improvement." Here he reiterates, in considerable detail, his philosophy and his ideas for the grounds of the state university.[42] The "scheme" accompanying it is clearly Hall's preliminary plan for these grounds,[43] and can, through close examination, be identified as the incomplete drawing drafted in ink on white linen now in the Bancroft Library (Figure 5).[44] The plan is incomplete in that it lacks any trees, except along the streets, and has neither a title block, scale, north arrow, nor date. A note in soft pencil on this plan, apparently added later, states "Plan for the Cal. University Grounds Berkeley - Made by Wm. Ham Hall 1874 - Copy sent to Mr. Olmsted and he acknowledged by letter dated Mar 23d 1874." It is likely that this identification is incorrect, since by that date Hall would have sent Olmsted a copy of his final plan.

The level of detail shown in the plan and discussed in his letter makes one wonder how and where Hall found the precedents for the site's eight principal structures, their sitings, functions, and interrelationships, and for the other university facilities. Although Olmsted's 1866 report may have provided Hall with some general guidance, it does not provide, as noted earlier, the same level of detail of his own report. Another source might be the previously noted proposal from the architectural firm of Wright and Sanders, sent to the regents in July 1869. It is, however, more concerned

---

[40]Hall to Gilman, June 2, 1873 (Hall papers, Bancroft Library).

[41]Albert G. and Mary Dornin Pickerell, *The University of California, A Pictorial History* (Berkeley, 1968), 15.

[42]Hall to Gilman, June 2, 1873 (Hall papers, Bancroft Library).

[43]William Hammond Hall, *Plan for the Cal. University Grounds Berkeley - Made by Wm. Ham Hall 1874 (sic)* . . . , map, probably May 1873 (University Archives, H3/Case XD). (Hereafter: Hall, *Cal. Grounds.*)

[44]Hall, *Cal. Grounds.*

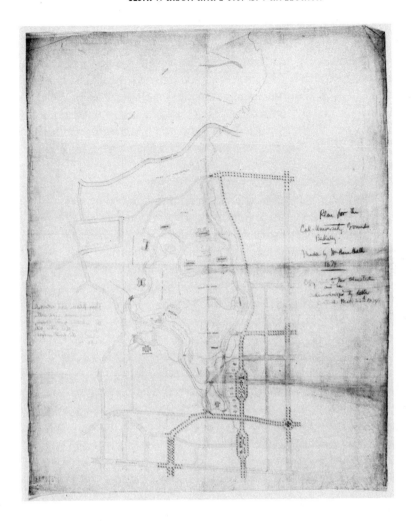

Figure 5: Hall's preliminary campus plan, 1873.

with the function and structure of each of the three main buildings than with their relationship to the grounds.[45]

Although Hall had noted in his letter that it was "necessary to totally disregard the work which has already been done in the way of road making and planting," he does allow the retention, with slight alteration, of most of the drive along the creek (Strawberry Creek) with its bridge connecting to the Felton property (Dana Street). Even "the tree planting already done, might be utilized temporarily, and gradually supplemented by a more thoughtful arrangement."[46]

Hall's four "requisites" for formulating the plan:

1. That the building sites which nature has provided be preserved for such purpose and set aside for the most appropriate occupation.

2. That suitable localities be designated for other specific purposes, and developed in a manner suited to such use.

3. That the general development of the grounds be such as will promote the convenient use of the principal elements of the institution, and enhance the natural beauty of the site, while introducing the artificial structures necessary for its profitable occupation.

4. And that economy of construction and maintenance be closely adhered to and planned for.

Except for the style of prose and the use of certain words, these might be the criteria for any well-conceived modern plan; yet they were written in 1873 by a 27-year-old self-trained "engineer" who had neither attended college nor was formally trained in planning or landscape design.

Hall describes the elements of the University:

I have supposed the future university to consist of a College of Sciences and Engineering, a College of Letters and Law, a School of Mines, a School of Medicine, a College of Agriculture, a Museum, a Library, and a Assembly Hall. . . . The Library [placed] where it will have room to spread to a vast size, very convenient of access from without the grounds . . . the Museum, also a growing institution, on a spot where it may be enlarged, adjacent to the School of Medicine and of Mines to which departments the greater

---

[45]Wright and Sanders, letter, July 6, 1869 (University Archives, Box 1, Folder 14).

[46]Hall to Gilman, June 2, 1873 (Hall papers, Bancroft Library).

portion of its contents will have some relation: while the College of Agriculture is located in the midst of the grounds allotted to the experimental illustration of the pursuits of which the theory is therein taught; and the Assembly Hall upon the most pleasing inviting site, retired, yet the most accessible from the two main carriage entrances, and from the depot of the horse cars without.

The need to locate faculty residences near to, but not as part of, the "main grouping" of the other campus facilities prompted Hall, apparently heeding a suggestion, to find the southwest corner of the site to be "most fitting for the purpose." There he could develop an "arrangement of the lots and houses fronting upon a little park" yet accessible to the city street where the rear entrances and walks would be screened from view "from the main grounds by plantations following the general line of the back walks."

Hall gives five reasons for this location:

(1) the impropriety of bringing into the groupings of structures in the main portions of the grounds and elements so foreign to the general tone of the establishment, (2) opportunity for drainage and sewerage at small expense, (3) facility with which rear yards and offices [i.e., privies] may be excluded from view, (4) accessibility by commercial travel, thus excluding . . . a very undesirable class of vehicles . . . (5) greater neighborhood conveniences and ease of access to the occupants of the houses therefrom.

Finally, Hall wrote that when a chapel "becomes part of the institution the proper place for it is in the quiet and accessible valley near the main entrance as indicated." Although a building is shown on this site in the final plan, it is neither identified nor is it described in Hall's later, detailed report to the regents.

Hall seems to have been full of projects in 1873: two days before he submitted this preliminary plan on June 2, he responded positively to a suggestion by President Gilman that he consider serving as a lecturer "on the subject of Landscape Engineering."[47] Nothing further on this matter was found, but we know that on June 25, he wrote to "Friend" M. G. King, another civil engineer, about a joint surveying and mapping project in the

---

[47]Hall to Gilman, May 31, 1873 (Hall papers, Bancroft Library).

Berkeley neighborhood adjacent to the campus.[48] Similarly, on the same day he wrote President Gilman offering to perform the Berkeley surveying work (the University owned much of the adjacent property) in conjunction with the campus project.[49] John B. Felton, a Berkeley property owner and University regent, received an offer from Hall in July to prepare a Berkeley neighborhood plan,[50] and in August Hall informed Gilman of a property line dispute with a resident living adjacent to the campus.[51] As for his campus plan, Hall apparently received some comments on his preliminary plan over the next few months prompting some changes that he made before submitting his final plan later that year, sometime after November 30.

THE CAMPUS PLAN: THE FINAL PLAN

This was an elaborate and attractively drafted and rendered plan for the entire grounds of the University (comprising some 150 acres at that time.) (Figure 6) The document, now in two equal pieces, having evidently been torn at the fold, measures 50 inches high by 29.5 inches wide. It was drafted in ink on a thick presentation-style paper at a ratio of 1:2,000 (even though the map erroneously indicates 1:10,000) or 1" = 166.67 feet). North is to the left margin, and existing and proposed buildings are shown with shadows based upon the sun being in the northeast quadrant. Groves of trees are shown throughout the site with appropriate shadows, and even though the map is darkened with age, the green (ink or watercolor?) wash used to differentiate the groves from the ground plane is still visible.[52] In general the plan arranges the requisite colleges in buildings, on separate sites, in a roughly circular fashion connected by a loop road. In addition to the Colleges of Agriculture (South Hall) and Letters (North

---

[48]Hall to M. G. King, June 25, 1873 (WHH letterbook, Vol. 1, California Historical Society Library, San Francisco) 31-i2. (Hereafter: Hall to recipient, date (CHS Library).) Since only a few of Hall's own letters were found, I found it necessary to transcribe relevant letters from Hall's own letterbooks housed at the California Historical Society Library in San Francisco. My research was cut short by closure of the library, due to lack of funding, in early April 1989. The library has since reopened.

[49]Hall to Gilman, June 25, 1873 (Hall papers, Bancroft Library).

[50]Hall to John B. Felton, Esq., July 10, 1873 (CHS Library), 41-43.

[51]Hall to Gilman, August 2, 1873 (CHS Library), 68-69.

[52]Hall, *Proposed Plan*.

Hall), already in place, Hall identifies building sites for a Library, an Assembly Building, a Museum, a School of Mines building, a Horticulture building, and an unidentified building that we learn from his report is the School of Engineering and Mechanic Arts. Of particular importance for a university chartered as a Morrill Act land-grant college of agriculture and the mechanic arts, is the inclusion of substantial acreage for agricultural purposes. The northwestern quadrant is designated for an arboretum, economic botany, pomoculture, horticulture, and experimental and practical agriculture. Botanical gardens are more centrally located near North Hall.

The long note beginning on the lower left side of the plan highlights the plan's principal features:

This plan is based upon the shape of the grounds as represented from the topographic survey made by Cleveland Rockwell of the U.S. Coast Survey and the scale is the same as adopted for the topographical map. The roads, walks and other features here represented are intended to fit closely the curvature of the grounds thus avoiding any considerable cutting and filling in their construction, so that by far the greater portion of earthwork to be done in carrying out this plan is represented in the formation of the terraces about the Colleges of Agriculture and Letters. The fact that the institution is one of learning is held in view in the formation of this plan for the development of its grounds. Practical examples of many important engineering works, such as the construction of roads, bridges, culverts, archways, sub- and surface drainage, sewerage and distributing waterworks are afforded amongst its [continued, lower right-hand corner] details; while every facility for the varied studies of agriculture and of forestry, the arboretum, the grounds for economic botany, horticulture, floriculture, pomoculture, and experimental farming, is provided, and the allotment of grounds for the several special departments as the arrangement of details in each is made with reference to the landscape effect of the whole as well as the practical appropriateness [sic] of the specific tracts.

Furthermore, the variety which is afforded by the introduction of the terraces around the Colleges of Letters and Agriculture, aside from being the proper aesthetic treatment for the setting of these structures presents an opportunity for the exercise of the highest type of landscape gardening—this successful blending of the artificial with the natural, and insures on the site a complete example of the art of improving grounds according to landscape principles.[53] The plan, and final report submitted three months later in February, make it is clear that to create something artistic while addressing the practical needs of an institution for teaching agriculture and the mechanical arts, Hall had been influenced by his readings. For while the curvilinear paths reflect the principles found in the references suggested by Olmsted, especially the plans for the various large Paris parks reproduced in Robinson's *Parks & Promenades of Paris*, much of the grounds are simply set aside for practical, particularly agricultural, pursuits.

Hall's plan, however, was not unanimously accepted by those whom it would affect. In a six-page letter to Gilman on November 21, Hall "reluctantly answer[s] the objections" to his plans raised by Professor Ezra S. Carr.[54] Carr, appointed the professor of agriculture for the new university in 1869, had stated in a letter to Gilman on November 19, his objection to the grading of the terrace around the agricultural building (South Hall), and suggested that the current plan was not what "Mr. Olmsted" had in mind in his 1866 plan.[55]

In a later letter, November 30, to Gilman, Hall assumed that the work to implement his plan "should be done during the present Winter, the succeeding Spring, and Summer," though it could extend over four to six years. He estimated that the total cost of construction would be from 40,000 to 45,000 dollars, and he concludes: "I am engaged in making a drawing of the plan already submitted and will send it to you as soon as possible."[56] From this statement one can assume that the final plan, the subject of this essay, is the drawing titled "Proposed Plan for the Improvement of the Site of the University of California" and dated 1873. (Figure 6) It appears, therefore, that the rendered campus plan was finally submitted very soon after this last, November, letter.

---

[53]*Ibid.*

[54]Hall to Gilman, November 21, 1873 (CHS Library), 87-92.

[55]Ezra S. Carr, letter to D. C. Gilman, November 19, 1873 (University Archives, Box 1, Folder 5).

[56]Hall to Gilman, November 30, 1873 (CHS Library), 99-101. Also in *Biennial Report of the Secretary to the Regents* (Berkeley, 1874), 40-41.

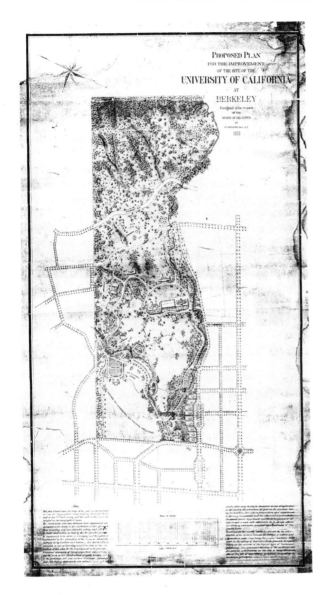

Figure 6: Hall's final plan, 1873-74.

THE CAMPUS PLAN: THE FINAL REPORT

Reading the detailed, nine-page (typeset) report addressed to the regents and the president, of February 1874, we can today appreciate the thought that Hall must have given to this undertaking and his respect for the existing landscape as the basis of the composition. (Appendix) The report also reflects his great admiration for, and deference to, the professional stature of Olmsted, "the accomplished Landscape engineer," and to Olmsted's plan for the same site; but Hall was not going to repeat it. In one of his several references to Olmsted's report (the plan having been lost), he says that although the needs of the earlier, smaller College were addressed in appropriate fashion, that now the land was intended for "a UNIVERSITY, and that the entire site should be occupied for such purpose."[57]

Thus the present plans for improvement are based upon an idea totally different from that upon which Mr. Olmsted formed his scheme; involving the conception of the entire area of one hundred and fifty acres [not the 35 acres in Olmsted's plan] manipulated as one educational institution—the material University.

Hall made a "renewed study of the subject; substituting for the idea of [Olmsted's] rural town, the conception of an educational park . . . so far as nature will permit the development of such elements." Gently rebuking the misguided efforts of others who had been at work on the campus, Hall "found it expedient to disregard, in a great measure, certain partial improvements, in the way of grading for roadways, as well as much of the planting of trees, executed during the interim, and which have evidently not been done according to any well considered plan."

In his report Hall repeats, often nearly verbatim, much of his earlier detailed proposal of June 1873 to President Gilman, including the four criteria and the description of the building sites. However there are several changes: the College of Agriculture has been relocated to one of the two existing buildings (South Hall), and its previous location has become the "School of practical Agriculture and Horticulture . . . located in the midst of the grounds allotted to the experimental pursuit of its course," as a result the College of Science designation has been removed from South Hall and does

---

[57]Hall, "Report of an Engineer Upon the Development of the Grounds at Berkeley," February 21, 1874, in *Report to the Regents* (Berkeley, 1874), 57-65. Appendix A (Hereafter: Hall, "Report.") See Appendix, p. 41.

not appear on the final plan. Also, the former "Medicine" building now labeled "Building Site," must be the "School of Engineering and Mechanic Arts" that Hall describes in the final report. Another intriguing addition is the house site for the "Professor of Agriculture," overlooking the horticultural grounds along the northern boundary of the campus. This possibly was a move by Hall to placate the opposition of Professor Carr to his plan.

Beyond Carr's own personal complaints about the plan, however, there was a growing controversy regarding the purpose and goals of the University. The challenge confronting President Gilman was to satisfy the need for a reputable institution for research and higher learning while addressing the farm lobby's complaint that practical agriculture was being overlooked.[58] Hall refers to this challenge in a March 1874 letter to Olmsted: "this 'statement of the Regents' has been compiled to refute certain attacks upon the management of the institution, made by 'Grangers' of our state."[59] From Hall's proposal, his letters, the plans and this detailed report, however, it is apparent that he responded to both sides of the controversy.[60]

In his description of the botanical-horticultural facilities Hall, as in his earlier report, combines the aesthetic with the practical, mentioning

A Conservatory, wherein much botanical knowledge can best be acquired, and always a pleasing and attractive feature . . . where it will present a remarkably fine effect in the principal landscapes. This feature, and the surrounding rich garden, the space devoted to Economic Botany—a low valley well adapted to the purpose—and the horticultural grounds on the table land above, are all adjacent to the nursery and propagating houses, from whence they will be in a measure supplied with stock.

In this final report Hall expands his narrative to include discussions on the principles of landscape composition, and on the roads, walkways, and campus gateways, and closes with over two pages devoted to "the terraces around the Colleges of Agriculture and Letters, now in course of construction"—no doubt a defensive response to Carr's complaints.

In the section devoted to the roads, walkways, and gateways of the campus, Hall's sensitive treatment of landscape is apparent: "The University grounds must not be regarded as a driving park" since "such a presumption

---

[58]Ferrier, *Origin*, 355.
[59]Hall to FLO, March 12 or 13, 1874 (CHS Library), 151.
[60]Hall, "Report." See Appendix.

would soon bring about a use of them highly detrimental to the real object of the institution." "Roads," he continues, "must be regarded as necessary evils in the University grounds, and only located where desirable to approach its principal features. The least measure of roadway to answer this requirement is the proper amount to be planned." Furthermore, while respecting the natural topography, maintaining easy grades, and avoiding earthwork, the road widths should be

> just sufficient to answer the purposes of maximum travel—from twenty to twenty-five feet—touching upon the points required to be approached by vehicles, and an observance of the rules of tasteful landscape gardening, with the requisites of good engineering principles. . . .

The layout of the walks, connecting only principal structures "except . . . where it is desirable to awaken some special interest by the development of parterres, devoted to ornamental as well as instructive horticulture and floriculture," followed Hall's own fourth criterion of "economy of construction and maintenance."

Gateways, he writes, should be limited since "a multiplication of them increases cost of maintenance, and destroys the air of security and seclusion which these grounds should have." Therefore, he shows only two each on the north and south sides, and one on the west. He admonishes against locating the main entrance at the end of University Avenue "a most unfitting place, upon the side of a hill, necessitating a steep grade to surmount, or a sharp curve to avoid it, and otherwise violating the established rules of good taste and engineering."

> The main entrance to the University should be spacious, commensurate with the dignity of the institution, and in keeping with general air of the grounds. The valley where I have located it admits of this treatment; the end of University Avenue, as projected, does not.

Hall's map shows a single entrance just north of the current Center Street entrance; the University Avenue proposal condemned by Hall was later implemented in a somewhat different fashion.

Going on to the provision for agricultural and botanical facilities, Hall, to counteract the pressures being applied by the Grangers and their allies, cites "the principles of landscape composition" that "should govern in a great measure the arrangement of these grounds," but "the fact the institution is one of learning should be held in view in the development of every

28

portion of the lands; [and] *the entire conversion of this beautiful site into a school of practical horticulture and agriculture would be a needless act of vandalism* [emphasis added]." Furthermore, Hall "would make [the botanical studies areas] arrangement subservient to principles governing the effect of the whole, and not a mere carrying out of botanical classification."

The last part of Hall's report is devoted to justifying the other policy attacked by agriculture professor Carr, the creating of terraces around the North and South Halls. As advocates for the earlier Olmsted plan, Carr and his supporters erroneously assumed that Hall was violating an Olmsted principle by not bringing the natural landscape right up to the buildings. They evidently based their assumption only on Olmsted's schematic plan and not reading his report. Hall, however, meticulously articulates his rationale for their use. After describing the buildings as "massive structures, set upon a formal frontage line on the gently sloping surface of a flat spur of the hills," he continues, "public buildings, from their stately character, obviously demand the most formal settings; and none require greater space in this treatment than those to be frequented by crowds of college boys."

His plan introduces elements "which will heighten the effect of the rural air of the grounds, by imparting a breadth of foreground, a charm of variety, and a contrast of decorative art with the beauties of nature." Therefore, the principal effect of the building terraces, when seen from the west "will be to impart a dignity, a sense of security and stability to the structures, which the preservation of the natural slope would have defeated."

Hall wanted to remove the "hummock of earth" that existed between the two buildings in order to allow the ground line of one building to be viewed from the other, and to use the material thus generated for terraces and roads. He indicates that "the ground in the rear will be sloped back into the present fall of the hill, so as to have a perfectly natural appearance on this side of the building." Using rather uncharacteristically colorful similes, he attacks his critics: to have the natural treatment right up to the building bases "would have been as appropriate as the location of a castellated Gothic structure in the middle of a wide plain, or the construction of a fancy woodwork foot bridge at the base of the Yosemite Falls." Similarly, the construction of the terraces will satisfy the need for "some small area of well-kept ground" thus "avoiding the appearance which the building would otherwise have—of a couple of fine structures in the middle of a ploughed field."

Since Carr had invoked the legacy of the Olmsted plan, Hall wisely repeats Olmsted's own words to support his own position, quoting from his mentor's 1866 report: "The central buildings are intended to be placed upon an artificial plateau at the head of the dell before described. . . . The west front of this plateau is designed to take the form of an architectural terrace." To further the argument Hall includes another full paragraph from Olmsted in which "the terrace may be finished very plainly and cheaply," but at the same time allow "the introduction of a high degree of art at any time in the future," that is, improvements such as statues, fountains, and decorative pavements. Concluding this discussion, Hall reasserts the similarity of his and Olmsted's treatment of the terraces, a similarity that he was glad to emphasize by quoting Olmsted's reference.

Ending his report, Hall refers again to the importance of the grounds: "[t]here is probably no established University in the world, whose grounds take so prominent a part in the general educational system of the institution as those at Berkeley may be made to perform, by a judicious system of development." Once the design is fixed, its execution "will afford [the students] valuable practical examples of the theories taught in the agricultural, engineering, and mechanical courses of study of the institution," and although the complete development of the grounds, "after the primary works are finished, may be prolonged through a series of years . . . the works necessary for the pleasurable and profitable occupation of the grounds [should] be executed at once."

These works would cost "at least fifteen or twenty thousand dollars for each of the succeeding two years." The higher cost estimate, compared to the 40,000 to 45,000 dollars over a period of four to six years mentioned in his letter to Gilman of November 30, is possibly due to the greater detail Hall had at this point and the additional time available to be more precise in his preparation of the estimate.

The completion of this report and submission of the plan seems to have concluded Hall's official duties on behalf of the regents, even though their approval was yet to come. On March 12 or 13, 1874, however, Hall seeks Olmsted's support and counsel in a six-page letter.[61] He writes first of the ongoing funding problems with the Golden Gate Park project, then refers to the need for a rustic carpenter at the park site, and asks for a reference for "a landscape architect" from Chicago seeking employment. He tells Olmsted of the transmittal of his Berkeley report along with "a photograph of the plan I have submitted" and then writes of his difficulties, previously

---

[61]Hall to FLO, March 12 or 13, 1874 (CHS Library), 151.

mentioned, in completing it. Hall expresses the hope that Olmsted's "former connection with these grounds is . . . done justice to in this report" although they come from widely different standpoints in viewing the project. He again vents some frustration with the "Grangers": "These people would have the University turned into a labor school, and its ground devoted to turnip, gooseberry and cabbage experimental rows. What the upshot of it all will be I know not."

Although he had seen only Olmsted's report and not his plan, since it had apparently been lost, Hall explains that he felt it expedient to quote from Olmsted in order to "answer to one of my critics—the wife of the professor of Agriculture, who affects landscape gardening" and had "written in denunciation of my terraces." He then concludes:

> I am accused of all sorts of extravagancies and vagaries in my plans and all to get these grounds into the hands of an old professor of Agriculture who does not know the first principle of improving them. What [do] you think of my plans so far as you can judge them from [a] picture and report with your knowledge of the grounds?

Olmsted's response, in a March 23, 1874, letter to Hall, seems more like a respectful critique than a complete endorsement, even though it supports Hall's views over those of his critics.[62] Noting that Hall's apparent axial line is in a different location from his, the former following a ridge, the latter, his own, lying along a valley, Olmsted sees "an obvious difference of motive here between the two plans." He goes on to suggest that if he were to prepare a plan for the site under Hall's instruction he would depart even further "from the natural picturesque in landscape gardening" than Hall has done:

> [my views] are that the principles of English landscape gardening, which in this [East Coast] climate I am disposed to carry to a greater extreme than they have ever been carried in Europe, are out of place in the climate of California. I should seek to cover the ground mainly with anything by which I could secure a simply inoffensive low tone; not unnatural, never, suggesting death or constant labor to keep alive. I should consequently have much less

---

[62]FLO to WHH, March 23, 1874, Hall papers, Bancroft Library. (Figure 7.)

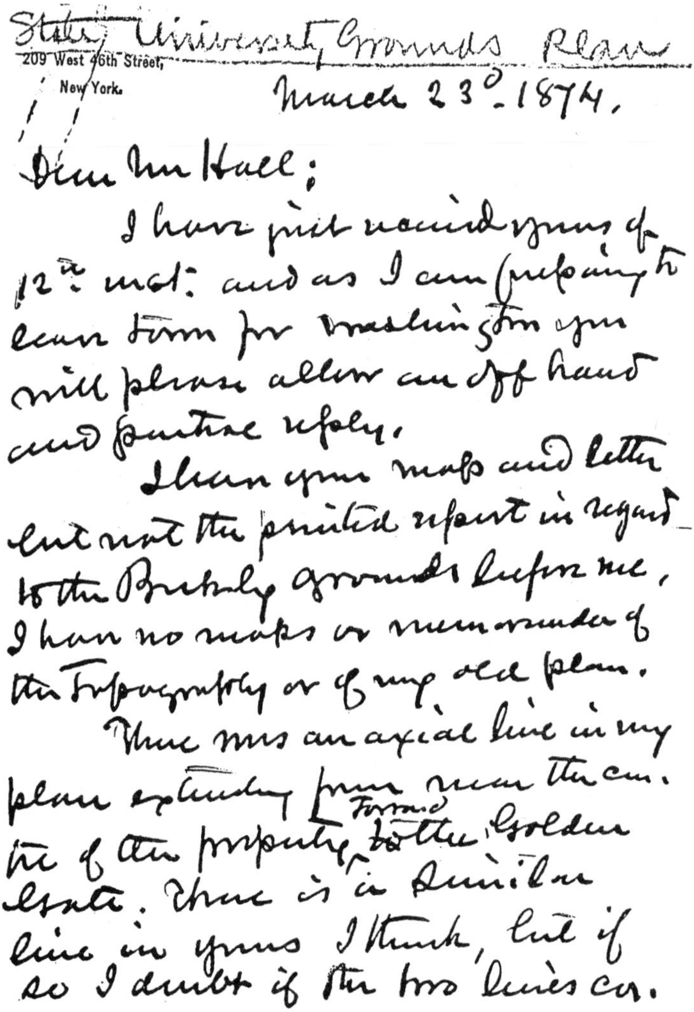

State University Grounds Plan

209 West 46th Street,
New York.

March 23º 1874.

Dear Mr Hall;

I have just received yours of 12th inst: and as I am preparing to leave town for Washington you will please allow an off hand and positive reply.

I have your map and letter but not the printed report in regard to the Berkeley grounds before me. I have no maps or memoranda of the Topography or of my old plan.

There was an axial line in my plan extending from near the centre of the property, Formed to the Golden Estate. There is a similar line in yours I think, but if so I doubt if the two lines are.

Figure 7: Letter from Frederick Law Olmsted to W. H. Hall, March 23, 1874.

Respect for the present minor/natural features, *for wherever you put foliage in broad dense bodies you obliterate the old nature as effectively as if you had laid it out with bricks and mortar* [emphasis added]. I should accentuate the brightness, cheerfulness and elegance on a few plainly artificial elements, such as terraces, avenues and parterres, strictly formal and as unquestionably artificial as a necklace or bracelet. You do less in this way than I should wish to do.

From this discussion Olmsted seems to assume that Hall intended his open spaces to be treated as "English lawns," even though Hall neither indicates such a treatment on his plan nor includes a description of the groundcovers in his report. In fact, the implication to be drawn from Hall is that only the building terraces would be so treated as they will satisfy the need for "some small area of well-kept ground."

Olmsted does defer to Hall's position as the resident professional, adding: "But you know that I should submit my views with great respect for the immeasurable advantage that you have gained in your much longer, closer, most special and practical study of the conditions in their bearing upon our common art." He asks Hall to show President Gilman his letter "or better, tell him from me that I could not be as bold as you in attempting English lawn effects in the climate of California, except in the smallest work," and concludes: "I should wish to go much further than you propose to do in humble following of types which many centuries ago were enjoyed and accepted gratefully by artists in comparison with whom all now living are pygmies." Does he imply only that that their current collective efforts as landscape designers pale in comparison to those of their ancient predecessors, or that Hall is insufficiently modest?

Olmsted's abruptness and an apparent lack of understanding of Hall's detailed treatment can be ascribed to his occupation with other more pressing matters. Even so, the two continued to correspond over the years. They may have finally met in October 1886 when Olmsted journeyed to the West, some 15 years after Hall began the correspondence. Even though Olmsted visited Golden Gate Park, there is no clear evidence that a meeting occurred.[63]

---

[63]Roper, *FLO*, 408.

THE CAMPUS PLAN:
APPROVAL AND IMPLEMENTATION

Although other campus plans existed before 1874, evidence uncovered for this essay shows Hall's plan to have been the primary one during the ensuing 25 years. First, that Hall's plan enjoyed official recognition is apparent from the inclusion of his complete report in the 1874 *Report of the Secretary to the Regents of the University of California* (Appendix). Then, on April 9, 1874, a Special Committee of the Board of Regents passed a resolution to adopt and implement Hall's plan, and at a special meeting on April 22, the regents adopted the committee's report.[64] Included in the board's final action was the statement that Hall should work with the engineering faculty in implementing the plan.

Following this April 1874 adoption, however, although the University's archives contain a number of descriptive references to various improvements being undertaken and paid for, few concrete references to Hall's plan could be found. One exception is a letter two years later from Frank Soulé, Jr., professor of civil engineering and astronomy. On May 16, 1876, he wrote to the Board of Regents stating that he had no prior knowledge of the board's instructions to work with Hall in implementing Hall's plan.[65] No other reference to any working relationship between the two engineers was found.

Nonetheless, by reviewing the various maps that were produced for the campus between 1874 and 1897, one can see that substantial parts of Hall's plan were indeed executed. For example, Professor Soulé, in 1875, prepared a drawing entitled *Map of Strawberry Valley and Vicinity, Showing the Natural sources of the Water Supply of The University of California. . . .*[66] This map uses Hall's plan as the base map for the location of various pipes, etc. on the main campus.

On the Soulé map each of the numbered campus buildings, identified in a legend, called "Explanations," corresponds with one of Hall's. They are Library, Museum site, Building site, School of Mines, Conservatory;

---

[64]Hall, "Report." Regents, Special Committee Resolution (April 9, 1874): Special Committee Minutes (April 13, 1874); Minutes of Special Meeting (April 22, 1874), University Archives.

[65]Frank Soulé, Jr., letter to regents, May 16, 1876 (University Archives).

[66]Soulé, *Map* (University Archives, 1875).

"&c," Nursery, Horticulture, and Assembly Hall. Soulé's map has the "Main Entrance to Grounds" in the same location as Hall, while the "student quarters," along the southwestern boundary, appear to be the structures that Hall proposed as faculty residences. Both maps show the no longer existent central branch of Strawberry Creek.

A review of other campus maps between 1875 and 1897 further substantiates Hall's influence on the development of the grounds. Although between 1875 and 1882 only two maps, depicting only minor additions were found (perhaps due to the relatively slow growth of the campus during this period), beginning in 1882 a series of larger scale, more detailed maps of the campus were prepared.

Malcolm G. King, the civil engineer with whom Hall had corresponded in 1873, prepared a boundary map entitled *Map of the State University Tract, Berkeley, Alameda Co., Cal.*, surveyed March 1882, at the scale of 1:2,000 (1" = 166.67').[67] Since this is the same scale that Hall used for his plan, the two maps can be overlaid and compared. Allowing for normal discrepancies in drafting and the differences in media used, the two plans bear a striking similarity. Both the Harmon Gymnasium (built 1879), occupying the site of the proposed Assembly building, and the Bacon Art and Library Building (built 1881) are located almost exactly where Hall had proposed. The Mechanic Arts Building (built 1879), however, is approximately 175 feet southeast of the "Building Site" location selected by Hall. Behind (east of) the latter building are two identical laboratory buildings. In Hall's plan the connecting roadway from the main buildings, south of the gymnasium, to the bridge at the Dana Street entrance, can also be seen in the King map, but passing the gymnasium on the north.[68] An unattributed map, rather crudely drawn, entitled "Sketch of University Grounds" (no date), at the scale of 1" = 500'. As it covers the entire campus area, we see for the

[67]Malcolm G. King, *Map* (University Archives, 1882).

[68]Another map by King, *Plan* (University Archives, 1884), finely drafted in ink on linen, depicts the *Plan of improvements at the State University showing roads opened and improved in the year 1884*. In 1885 R. C. Turner and H. I. Randall produced a highly detailed map that shows for the first time an axial walkway leading from the main buildings towards the Golden Gate (*Contour map of a portion of the State University Tract to be improved 1885-86.: Berkeley, Cal. Surveyed June, 1885*, University Archives, 1885).

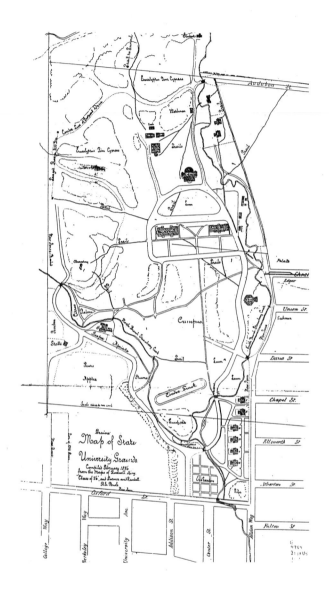

Figure 8: R. E. Bush, map of Campus, 1886.

first time the inclusion of improvements for the "Botanical Gardens" in the same general area that Hall had proposed.[69]

In February 1886 R. E. Bush compiled a map entitled *Map of State University Grounds* from the maps of Rockwell (the topographic survey map Hall had used) King, "Class of '86," and Turner and Randall.[70] (Figure 8) As a compilation of maps from that period, it is a helpful documentation of how much of Hall's plan had been implemented in the intervening 12 years. From the notes on this map we see that most of Hall's areas for "Pomoculture, Horticultural Grounds and Grounds for Economic Botany" had been established (see areas designated by Bush for pears, apples, grapes, apricots, and plums). The "Hot Houses" are approximately 75 feet north of the site Hall had chosen for his "Nursery" buildings, near the prominent crook in the North Branch of Strawberry Creek. Also, another of Hall's features, the roadway system connecting these areas to a lower campus entrance has been installed, although Hall had proposed a more pleasing curvilinear alignment for the entrance road. The now well-known Eucalyptus grove near the confluence of the two branches of Strawberry Creek was in place by this time, along with a cinder track to the east (built 1886).

By 1897, on a highly detailed map by the College of Civil Engineering, we see the Engineering Building very close to Hall's "Site for Museum."[71] The road system, too, in the vicinity of this building, is similar. The Botanical Garden, now quite extensive, extends from near Hall's proposed site westward to the area he designated for the Arboretum. Also, the Conservatory is within two hundred feet of the one on Hall's plan.

AN ASSESSMENT OF HALL

From the above review it is apparent that Hall's 1873 plan heavily influenced the layout of the various campus improvements during the ensuing 25 years. Why has he not been more fully recognized for his

---

[69]Although filed as an 1885 (University Archives) map, it appears to be much later since it shows improvements not seen on the February 1886 map, such as a "Plant H." (conservatory) and "Chem" building.

[70]R. E. Bush, *Map* (University Archives, 1886).

[71]University of California, College of Civil Engineering, *Grounds and Buildings of the University of California, Berkeley: Alameda County, California, U.S.A.* (University Archives, San Francisco, 1897).

contributions? One can only speculate that since he was not a dominant presence at Berkeley during these years—he was busy building Golden Park until 1876—he was not readily available to defend his plan. Also, his heritage, politics, and personality may have affected his recognition. He was a southerner by birth and a Democrat, two facts that may not have been lost upon the northern-sympathizing Republicans who tended to be in power. It has been said that Hall has difficulty fitting into the establishment dominated by Union sympathizers.[72] Furthermore, "[Hall was f]ar from tactful, he had little regard for the value of compromise. . . . He found it impossible to see how any man or group could not see the wisdom of his plans," and so became "most certainly an example of the neglected prophet."[73]

Then too, Hall's career as a civil engineer was on the rise. His interest and expertise in irrigation and water use in California led to his appointment in 1878 by Governor William Irwin as the first state engineer, a post that he held until it was abolished by the legislature in 1888. As state engineer he authored several seminal reports on irrigation, and in 1889 he was appointed the supervising engineer for the United States Irrigation Survey, the predecessor of the U.S. Reclamation Service.[74]

Beginning in 1890, when he opened his private practice as a civil engineer, Hall worked on a variety of irrigation and hydroelectric projects in California and Washington. For the next 10 years he undertook similar projects in such far-flung places as Europe, Russia, and South Africa, where he advised Cecil Rhodes. In 1900 he returned to California and was chiefly engaged in property management for investment and development, including the acquisition of Lake Eleanor and Cherry Creek watersheds in Tuolumne County, which he subsequently sold to the City of San Francisco for its water supply. In 1905 Hall prepared a study on the proposed Panama Canal that convinced Senator George C. Perkins to advocate the lock system instead of a sea-level canal.[75]

---

[72]See note 4.

[73]Charles B. Korr, quoted by Larry Deblinger in "The Real Father of Golden Gate Park," in *This World*, 15-16, a section of *San Francisco Examiner & Chronicle* (San Francisco, August 27, 1989).

[74]Jones, "Hall," 11-12.

[75]*Ibid.*; *Examiner, Library*, 121.

During these years of work on a variety of engineering projects, Hall wrote articles defending the sanctity of his beloved Golden Gate Park as a public pleasure ground.[76] In his role as consulting civil engineer to the Board of Park Commissioners, he prepared a pamphlet against use of the park as a site for the 1915 Panama Pacific International Exposition. Concerned that it would commercialize this public ground, Hall, in July 1911 sent a copy of the pamphlet to James Sturgis Pray, chairman of the Harvard University Department of Landscape Architecture, seeking the latter's assistance in protecting the park from this threat. In his response, Pray commended Hall for his "strong stand," saying that it was "in line with what is best in this perennial conflict between those who generally appreciate the true functions of naturalistic parks and those who do not." He then suggested that Hall send a copy of his tract to the editors of *Landscape Architecture* (magazine) whom he felt would "be exceedingly glad to refer to your report as one of the most encouraging of recent statements."[77]

Hall's lifelong love for Golden Gate Park found an outlet in his unpublished manuscript "The Romance of a Woodland Park," written sometime before 1929, in which he detailed his struggles with nature and politicians to create the park and to maintain it as a refuge from city life, free from artificial intrusions.

Though much of Hall's campus plan was implemented, he wrote in discouragement in 1884 that "the work which has been done conforms only in generalities to the original plan drawn by me eight or nine years ago, and some abominable mistakes have been made in carrying it out."[78] Probably Hall discontinued his association with the University later that year.[79] Hall died in 1934 and is buried in Colma, California.[80]

WILLIAM HAMMOND HALL: LANDSCAPE ARCHITECT

William Hammond Hall was a landscape architect by whatever definition one wishes to employ. For example, the American Society of Landscape Architects in 1988 defined landscape architecture as "the

---

[76] Jones, "Hall," 12.
[77] James Sturgis Pray, letter to Hall, July 25, 1911 (University Archives).
[78] Bolton, "History," 16.
[79] *U.C. Chronicle* (1915), 106.
[80] Hall, "Romance." Jones, "Hall," 12.

profession which applies artistic and scientific principles to the research, planning, design and management of both natural and built environments." The profession's practitioners apply their skills and knowledge "in the planned arrangement of natural and constructed elements on the land with a concern for the stewardship and conservation of natural, constructed and human resources. The resulting environments shall serve useful, aesthetic, safe and enjoyable purposes."[81]

For his day, we can certainly say that Hall employed "artistic and scientific principles" to create "a useful, aesthetic, safe and enjoyable" environment for the Berkeley campus in 1873, and to create the first plan for Golden Gate Park.[82] Hall was able to visualize grand areas and to articulate the importance of large-scale planning. Although rather quaintly put, in an 1873 letter to Berkeley resident John Felton, Hall expressed his vision for the young city:

[the property owners must] recognize the importance of having a prefixed, harmonious scheme, based upon correct engineering and landscape principles and a due consideration of economy of subdivision of several tracts, for the development of a neighborhood destined to hold so important a position as Berkeley.[83]

Even though Hall went on to become an internationally known civil engineer, he maintained an affection and longing for landscape design, exemplified in his love for Golden Gate Park as expressed in "The Romance of a Woodland Park," which was dedicated to Frederick Law Olmsted and "his kindly personal advice by letters commencing years before I met him."[84] Hall clearly recognized Olmsted's role as mentor in forming his own skill and professionalism in the planning and design of the land resource. It is hoped that with this essay Hall's contributions can be given proper recognition, at last.

---

[81]American Society of Landscape Architects, *1988/89 Members Handbook* (Washington, 1988), 2.

[82]Commissioners, "Report," 27-38.

[83]Hall to Felton, July 10, 1873 (CHS Library), 41-43.

[84]Hall, "Romance," 1.

APPENDIX

Response to the fourth inquiry. Report of an Engineer upon the Development of the Grounds at Berkeley.

"Fourth. In response to the inquiry, the following Report in respect to the grounds is presented. It is drawn up by W. H. Hall, Esq., a most competent engineer, to whom the supervision of the work has been entrusted."

To The Honorable Board of Regents and President of the University of California:

Gentlemen.—In presenting the diagram, herewith transmitted, representing the plan I have proposed for the development of the University Grounds at Berkeley, I have deemed it expedient to call your attention to the circumstances connected with their past manipulation, and to review the leading ideas and features proposed to be embodied in their future improvement.

The first steps which were taken towards the improvement of these grounds, were made by its former managers—the Trustees of the College of California, a private corporation—who in 1865, obtained the services of Mr. Olmsted—the accomplished Landscape Engineer—then on a visit to California. This gentleman devoted much time and study to his subject, the results of which were embodied in a plan for the grounds, and a report, dated June 29th, 1866, in which the full aesthetic idea of the improvement is ably reviewed.

The College of California was a private corporation, which contemplated the establishment of a modest institution, chiefly of a classical and literary nature. Two buildings, at most, were to be erected. The site embraced over a hundred acres of land, and Mr. Olmsted was asked to prepare a plan for its improvement as a park. He called the attention of the Trustees to the fact, that the maintenance of such a ground, would be a burdensome tax upon their corporation; and advised them to create upon their ground a suburban residence neighborhood, reserving only sufficient space for College purposes, at most but thirty or thirty-five acres. His views were adopted, and his plans were formed to develop the grounds in a manner suitable for the purpose specified.

Subsequently, the land was deeded to the State, upon condition that on it should be established a University, and that the entire site should be occupied for such purpose. Features of other elements, merged into this institution, contemplated grounds for agricultural and horticultural operations, and the tract so donated afforded the requisite space. Thus the present plans for improvement are based upon an idea totally different from that upon which Mr. Olmsted formed his scheme; involving the conception of the entire area of one hundred and fifty acres manipulated as one educational institution—the material University. The plans prepared by Mr. Olmsted, therefore, were not available for the present institution, however much suited to the requirements of the College of California they may have been, or artistic and perfect for the formation of the contemplated suburban Home Grounds, as no doubt from, the well-known ability of the author, they were.

I have found it necessary, therefore, to make a renewed study of the subject; substituting for the idea of a rural town, the conception of an educational park, capable of being made complete in the requisite details of agricultural, horticultural, and general scientific study, so far as nature will permit the development of such elements. I have also found it expedient to disregard, in a great measure, certain partial improvements in the way of grading for roadways, as well as much of the planting of trees, executed during the interim, and which have evidently not been done according to any well considered plan.

Unfortunately, there is not that appreciation of the importance of prearranged and definite plans for such works, which there should be. The grounds around public buildings are regarded as immaterial accessories of the main architectural features, and not as settings to be the gems, which they really are; essential parts of an harmonious whole, suggestive of its character, in keeping with the design, and promotive of its convenient and effective use. All rational improvement of grounds is necessarily founded on a due attention to the character of the institution of which they form a part; upon a thorough study of the situation to be handled, and of the climatic and neighborhood influences to which it is subjected. The situation is, of course, a natural formation, to be adapted by Art to the uses required. The character of the institution governs the manipulation of the details of construction, in the grounds as well as the buildings; the allotment and adaptation of the various natural features to their specific purposes; while the climatic and neighborhood influences have an immediate and important effect upon the convenient and pleasurable use, as well as the successful improvement, of the demesne. All such improvements, however blessed by nature their site may be, must be regarded from their inception as works of Art. Nature does not provide lands shaped, and drained, and planted to suit the specific purposes of man. We are to seize her salient features, and allot them, as may be best, to our definite requirements; and, while preserving her more attractive spots in their integrity, develop an intricacy, a diversity of detail, presenting a succession of pleasing situations, varied in character, yet so arranged as to be in accord with each other.

The arrangement of these grounds constitutes something more than the laying out of avenues and the planting of trees. It is in reality the planning of the material University. Neither one nor all of the buildings which are to be placed there, make up this institution in its entirety. It comprises all within the boundaries of the tract, and must be regarded as one big structure, in which the several buildings, designed as they will be for different purposes, are as rooms or wings set aside to such specific uses; superior in importance, and requiring a greater share of study in their design it is true, but no more distinctive features to be considered than the botanic garden—for the scientific arrangement of the plants, the departments for the practice of horticulture and agriculture, or even the recreation grounds, the ramble in the woods, or the mere landscape effects. Of course, when these principal features—the main architectural works—are located, we have to adapt all else to them; but where such is not the case, a considerable amount of care may well be taken in properly placing them. We cannot, however, fix or describe the situation suitable for a house, without at the same time forming some idea of the structure suited to the situation; nor should we make an allotment of ground to any specific purpose, without considering whether such use is to be suited to the locality.

I proceed at once to a consideration of the requisites of a general plan for these grounds, and the attention they have received at my hands:

1. That the building sites which nature has provided be preserved for such purpose and set aside for the most appropriate occupation.
2. That suitable localities be designated for other specific purposes, and developed in a manner suited to such use.
3. That the general development of the grounds be such as will promote the convenient use of the principal elements of the institution, and enhance the natural beauty of the site, while introducing the artificial structures necessary for its profitable occupation.
4. And that economy of construction and maintenance be closely adhered to and planned for.

Taking the two colleges now completed as a nucleus, there are eight principal sites for large buildings. On this basis I have supposed the future University to consist of a College of Agriculture, a College of Letters, (the two buildings new completed) a School of Mines, a School of Engineering and Mechanic Arts, a Museum, a Library, an Assembly Hall, and a School of practical Agriculture and Horticulture; and so placed them, as indicated, on these sites, as would seem most fitting. The Library, an ever increasing element, in a locality where it will have room to spread to a vast size, very convenient of access from without the grounds, central to the college of Agricultural Science, Letters, and School of Engineering and Arts, the pursuit of the courses of study in which will most frequently necessitate reference to its volumes. The Museum, also a growing institution, on a spot where its building may be enlarged, adjacent to the Schools of Mines, and Engineering and Arts, to which departments a great portion of the contents will have some relation; while the School of practical Agriculture and Horticulture is located in the midst of the grounds allotted to the experimental pursuit of its course; and the Assembly Hall upon the most pleasing and inviting site, retired, yet the most accessible from the two main carriage entrances, and from the depot of the horse-cars without.

I have regarded the proper disposition of the residences of the members of the faculty as a most important element in the problem; the more so, that they are not properly features of the University itself, and should not appear in its main groupings. I find a site which had been suggested, at the southwest corner of the grounds, most fitting for the purpose; and have so developed a neighborhood as to render its occupation pleasurable and convenient, as the arrangement of the lots and houses fronting upon a little Park, and of the rear entrances and walks will indicate—the whole to be excluded from view, from the main grounds, by plantations following the general line of the back walks. Of the many reasons for this location and development, I mention several, viz: First. The impropriety of bringing into the grouping of structures in the main portion of the grounds an element so foreign to the general tone of the establishment. Second. Opportunity for drainage and sewerage at small expense. Third. Facility with which rear yards and offices may be excluded from view. Fourth. Accessibility by commercial travel, thus excluding the necessity for a very undesirable class of vehicles entering the grounds. Fifth. Greater neighborhood convenience, and ease of access to the occupants of the houses themselves.

A Conservatory, wherein much botanical knowledge can best be acquired, and always a pleasing and attractive feature, is located at a protected spot, where the ground about it is adapted to the cultivation of such plants and shrubs as would be appropriate in its neighborhood, and where it will present a remarkably fine effect in the principal landscapes. This feature, and the surrounding rich garden, the space devoted to Economic Botany—a low valley well adapted to the purpose—and the horticultural grounds on the table land above, are all adjacent to the nursery and propagating houses, from whence they will be in a measure supplied with stock. The public picnic ground remains as it is, remote and sheltered, and easily arrived at from without.

The University grounds must not be regarded as a driving-park. Such a presumption would soon bring about a use of them highly detrimental to the real object of the institution. Drives there will be, in abundance, in the neighborhood; one—the Piedmont Way—traversing the upper portion of the tract itself, and which I have carefully planned without connection with the roads of the University, in order that such roads will not be converted into thoroughfares between the low lands and the way above. Roads, therefore, must be regarded as necessary evils in the University grounds, and only located where desirable to approach its principal features. The least measure of roadway to answer this requirement is the proper amount to be planned. A strict adherence to the natural topography, maintaining very easy grades, and avoiding earthwork, with a width just sufficient to answer the purposes of maximum travel—from twenty to twenty-five feet—touching upon the points required to be approached by vehicles, and an observance of the rules of tasteful landscape gardening, with the requisites of good engineering principles, are the considerations which have influenced the location of these features, as embraced in my plan. Another reason for limiting the amount of roadway is found in the observance of the fourth requisite of a plan for the grounds—namely, economy of construction and maintenance. Roads are expensive to make, and expensive to keep in repair. This consideration is also applicable to walks; and therefore I have planned with a view of making these direct avenues of communication between the principal structures, as far as the restrictions indicated above would permit, except at several limited localities, where it is desirable to awaken some special interest by the development of parterres, devoted to ornamental as well as instructive horticulture and floriculture.

Gateways are offices requiring attention; a multiplication of them increases cost of maintenance, and destroys the air of security and seclusion which these grounds should have. Therefore, two carriage entrances on each [of] the north and south sides, with one upon the west, is all that is admissible. It was proposed to locate the main entrances at the end of University Avenue; a most unfitting place, upon the side of a hill, necessitating a steep grade to surmount, or a sharp curve to avoid it, and otherwise violating the established rules of good taste and engineering. The main entrance to the University should be spacious, commensurate with the dignity of the institution, and in keeping with the general air of the grounds. The valley where I have located it admits of this treatment; the end of University Avenue, as projected, does not.

Though the principles of landscape composition should govern in a great measure the arrangement of these grounds, the fact that the institution is one of learning should be held in view in the development of every portion of the lands; but the entire conversion of this beautiful site into a school of practical horticulture and agriculture would be a needless act of vandalism. I would therefore establish a series of botanical studies, grounds for economic botany, the culture of fruits, berries, and farm produce; a forestry, an arboretum and other instructive features, some of which are indicated, stocked with a variety of trees and shrubs; but I would make their arrangement subservient to principles governing the effect of the whole, and not a mere carrying out of botanical classification.

One other feature demands some attention; the terraces around the Colleges of Agriculture and Letters, now in course of construction.

These buildings are massive structures, set upon a formal frontage line on the gently sloping surface of a flat spur of the hills. They occupy about the sites selected by Mr. Olmsted for the two buildings contemplated for the old College of California, as near, at least as one can judge from the text of his report (the drawings not being at hand).

Public buildings, from their stately character, obviously demand the most formal settings; and none require greater space in this treatment than those to be frequented by crowds of college boys. The planning of this particular portion of the Berkeley improvement has been done with the view of providing suitable settings for these buildings, affording ample room for the throngs of scholars and their friends, who may be expected to congregate about them at times, and introducing elements which will heighten the effect of the general rural air of the grounds, by imparting a breadth of foreground, a charm of variety, and a contrast of the decorative art with the beauties of nature. Their principal effect, from the west, will be to impart a dignity, a sense of security and stability to the structures, which the preservation of the natural slope would have defeated.

The fact that a hummock of earth existed upon a hill between the two buildings, cutting off the view of one ground line from the other, has necessitated the execution of the earth work which is now in progress. The plan contemplates the removal of this unsightly protuberance, and the use of the material so obtained in the construction of the roads and terraces in front of the buildings; while the ground in their rear will be sloped back into the present fall of the hill, so as to have a perfectly natural appearance on this side of the buildings. The preservation of the original slope about these buildings, with a natural treatment of the grounds up to their bases, would have been about as appropriate as the location of a castellated gothic structure in the middle of a wide plain, or the construction of a fancy woodwork foot bridge at the base of the Yosemite Falls. There will certainly be some small area of well-kept ground at Berkeley. This I have rendered possible to restrict to a small extent by the construction of the terraces, which, being treated as such dressed ground, establish at once an appropriate limit to such treatment, thus enabling the expense of maintenance to be reduced to the least amount, and avoiding the appearance which the building would otherwise have—of a couple of fine structures in the middle of a ploughed field. In this connection, it may be well to mention, that the plan submitted by Mr. Olmsted for treatment of the grounds around the two buildings contemplated by the old College of California, which, as said before, were to be located in nearly the place now under consideration, was similar in general aesthetic style to that which I have adopted, as we gather from the following paragraphs quoted from his report:

"The central buildings are intended to be placed upon an artificial plateau at the head of the dell before described. The west front of this plateau is designed to take the form of an architectural terrace. At the foot of these walks appropriate entrances are provided from a carriage way."

"The construction of the necessary plateau will not be an expensive undertaking, as the working plan will show, and the terrace may be finished very plainly and cheaply. At the same time, the introduction of a high degree of art at any time in the future will be practicable, in the form of statues, fountains, and a highly decorated parapet with tile and marble pavement upon the terrace, and on each side of the broad walks, the intermediate quadrangle, and the stair and entrance way."

Though Mr. Olmsted's general plan for the grounds could not have been adapted to the wants of the University, his conception of the treatment immediately about the two central structures of his design, was evidently identical in aesthetic idea with that which I have adopted, and I gladly avail myself of the above quoted paragraph in further elucidation of the feature of the plans now submitted.

There is probably no established University in the world, whose grounds take so prominent a part in the general educational system of the institution as those at Berkeley may be made to perform, by a judicious system of development. After the general design is fixed, and its outlines laid upon the ground, the execution of its details, performed as they may be in a great measure by the students, will afford valuable practical examples of the theories taught in the agricultural, engineering, and mechanical courses of study of the institution.

The expense of executing the works embraced in the ground plan herewith submitted, will, of course, be governed by the style of the detail work undertaken, which could be made to cost much or little. The expending of these moneys, after the primary works are finished, may be prolonged through a series of years. It is expedient, however, that the works necessary for the pleasurable and profitable occupation of the grounds be executed at once; and for this purpose, at least fifteen or twenty thousand dollars for each of the succeeding two years, will be required.

Very Respectfully,
Your obedient servant,
Wm. Hammond Hall,
Engineer

San Francisco, February 21st, 1874.

THE UNIVERSITY AND THE
CONSTITUTIONAL CONVENTION OF 1878

by Peter S. Van Houten

ACKNOWLEDGMENTS & DEDICATION

This essay is dedicated to the memory of three men important to the history of the University of California in the 1870s who deserve the thanks of the generations that have come after them: Daniel Coit Gilman, Eugene Woldemar Hilgard, and Joseph Webb Winans. Regent Winans serving as chairman of the convention's Committee on Education, with great skill and dedication shepherded the section pertaining to the University through an often hostile convention. His efforts culminated in the last minute approval of a section that gave the University freedom from legislative interference, a freedom often cited as a reason for its future success.

This essay is also dedicated to the memory of my father, Wendell Van Houten, Berkeley class of 1924. His love of history, particularly that of the western United States is in my blood too.

I gratefully acknowledge the work of the staff of the Center for Studies in Higher Education. Janet Ruyle provided needed guidance and valued assistance. Center director and Berkeley classmate Sheldon Rothblatt performed a major editorial role in shaping this essay. His hand is very much in evidence and is greatly appreciated. Carroll Brentano was continuously generous in her support and encouragement while pushing the project to completion with helpful criticism and timely suggestions. I deeply appreciate the inclusion of my essay in this series of publications.

DEBATES AND PROCEEDINGS

OF THE

CONSTITUTIONAL CONVENTION

OF THE

STATE OF CALIFORNIA,

CONVENED AT THE CITY OF SACRAMENTO, SATURDAY, SEPTEMBER 28, 1878.

E. B. WILLIS AND P. K. STOCKTON,

OFFICIAL STENOGRAPHERS.

UNIV. OF
CALIFORNIA

Volume I.

SACRAMENTO:
STATE OFFICE, : : : : : J. D. YOUNG, SUPT. STATE PRINTING.
1880.

Figure 9: J. H. C. Bonté's (secretary to the regents, 1881-1896) copy of the *Debates and Proceedings of the Constitutional Convention*.

THE UNIVERSITY AND THE
CONSTITUTIONAL CONVENTION OF 1878-1879

Peter S. Van Houten

The University of California was created in 1868 by action of the state legislature as specified by the Organic Act. The constitution drawn up by the 1849 First Constitutional Convention was simple and brief. Its authors drew heavily on the relatively new constitution of Iowa and on those of other states, primarily New York. The article on education (Article IX) also was brief; it simply set forth a framework upon which the educational system could be established in a region experiencing tremendous growth and development. Section 4 of Article IX established the University Fund. It provided that any lands donated to California for higher education, as well as income derived from those lands, should be preserved for the use of a university as a permanent fund "for the promotion of literature, the arts and sciences."[1]

In some 30 years of statehood, California experienced exponential growth.[2] The population increased dramatically, reaching more than three-quarters of a million people after a start of approximately 100,000. Measured by new standards, the foundations of civil authority established in 1849 appeared in danger of collapse. Discontent was widespread and occasionally raucous, and the issues troubling Californians were both statewide and local, general and specific. Critics charged government with corruption and what appeared to be the excessive powers of the legislature. Other critics and reformers deplored the manipulation of the markets for stocks and bonds, and still others, especially urban workers, were troubled by competition from cheap labor represented by Chinese immigrants, increasingly the targets of bigots or workers involved in labor movement issues.[3] In July 1877, for example, a group of ruffians did considerable

---

[1]*Debates and Proceedings of the Constitutional Convention of the State of California, 1878-1879*, (Sacramento: State Office, 1880), 9.

[2]Carl Brent Swisher, *Motivation and Political Technique in the California Constitutional Convention, 1878-79* (Claremont, Calif., 1930), 6.

[3]Dudley T. Moorehead, "Sectionalism and the California Constitution," in *Pacific Historical Review* XII, No. 3 (September 1943): 291.

damage to the Chinese district in San Francisco.[4] The violence frightened many members of the community and led to the formation of the Committee of Public Safety reminiscent of the Vigilance Committee of some two decades earlier.[5]

By 1878 social and economic conditions had deteriorated to the point where the state's first constitution seemed inadequate. Public dissatisfaction with governmental bodies and officials consequently led to a movement to revise the constitution through the mechanism of a Second Constitutional Convention. Many Californians considered the legislature itself to be the major source of mischief in government, since efforts to achieve reform in matters such as control of the railroads and elimination of special-interest legislation had come to naught because of legislative inaction. Many citizens believed that the most effective way to make corrupt politicians act on the will of the public was to place limitations on the legislature and to provide for frequent expression of popular opinion at the ballot box. Short terms of office for governmental officials and popular control over governmental or quasi-governmental bodies were policies with considerable support from the laboring members of the electorate.

The University's position within California was hardly secure. Its Board of Regents could, in the eyes of voters, appear to somehow function outside the purview of democratic review and exist immune to public opinion. Similarly and relatedly, its teaching and curricula also could be considered insulated from public opinion or needs. A decade after its foundation, the University found itself under attack from the same sectors that were seeking controls on the state senate and assembly and also entangled in the quarrels of sharply divided political factions, each with different views as to how the University was to satisfy its obligations to California society.

However, although repeatedly criticized, attacked, and threatened, the University emerged from the Second Constitutional Convention firmly implanted in a new state constitution as almost a "fourth branch" of government. Only a minority of American state universities could claim to be similarly favored. The story of that political transformation is complicated, dramatic, and perhaps was unpredictable, but history has shown that the resulting changes have been of overwhelming importance to the welfare

---

[4]N. Ray Gilmore and Gladys Gilmore, *Readings in California History* (New York, 1966), 182-87.

[5]*Ibid.*, 187-94.

and development of the University of California, as well as to the entire state of which it is a part.

THE SOCIAL POLITICS OF CALIFORNIA

By October 1877 the discontented urban workers had formed a Workingmen's Party of California whose platform demanded the exclusion of the Chinese, the removal of government from the "hands of the rich," the end of monopoly land-holding, and the domination of public office by members of their party.[6] Under the ascendancy of the San Franciscan Dennis Kearney, the party's influence spread throughout the state, but Kearney's strategies paradoxically weakened and split the membership (*inter alia*, he made party officers ineligible for nomination to public office[7]); so much so in fact that Henry George, the famous agrarian reformer and editor of the *San Francisco Evening Post*, described the Workingmen's Party nominees to the Constitutional Convention from San Francisco as "men utterly ignorant and inexperienced."[8]

Even more upset with the political status quo than workers were the state's farmers and other residents of agricultural areas. They were ultimately more formidable than the urban laboring classes. The vast majority of California's voting population lived in rural and farming areas—mining districts still contained a sizeable but dispersed population—and their special grievances against the cities, as well as their political potential, were to give University of California supporters serious reason for concern during the convention. In the 1870s, only a minority of California's growing population lived in cities, and of these, the overwhelming portion resided in the City and County of San Francisco. Other major concentrations of population providing sources for delegates were in the East Bay and the Sacramento and San Joaquin valleys. Given the weight of southern California in the state's affairs today, it is surprising to remember that Los Angeles was the region's only real city. It then supported only 11,000 residents compared to some 200,000 in the rival city to the north.

---

[6]Ralph Kauer, "The Workingmen's Party of California," in *Pacific Historical Review*, XIII (September 1944): 280.

[7]*Ibid.*

[8]Henry George, "The Kearney Agitation in California," in Gilmore, *Readings*, 203-08.

The legality of the Constitutional Convention was established by an Enabling Act approved by the California Legislature in 1878. One hundred and fifty-two delegates were elected. Three represented each senatorial district, while eight were chosen at large from each congressional district. The delegates, in turn, elected a president and other officers, adopted operating rules, and approved the creation of over 30 standing committees with which to carry out the convention's business. The president in turn appointed the members of the various committees. To these committees were referred the proposed constitutional amendments and resolutions, but final consideration of these by the convention required the approval of the Committee of the Whole. Some 1,600 pages of minutes were compiled and printed, but the minutes of committees were not kept.

Henry George divided delegates into three major groupings: "First, the lawyers, who largely represented corporate interests; second, the 'Grangers,' who represented the ideas and prejudices of the farmers and the landholders; third, the Workingmen, bent on making capital for the new party, and desirous of doing something for the working class, without the slightest idea of how to do it."[9] While George probably was showing his resentment for not being a Workingmen's delegate (he had refused to take an oath to follow the party's bidding), his analysis and groupings are useful.[10] Cutting across George's divisions were the customary affiliations with the nation's two main political parties, Democrats and Republicans, as well as issues, opinions, loyalties, and sympathies that were not necessarily political in origin.

The political strategies of a three-fold division of the votes are familiar. Somehow three must be reduced to two, and one way is for two groups to join on the grounds that they share common objectives. Frightened by the Kearneyites and fearful that they might capture the convention, members of the two traditional parties, Democrats and Republicans, had partly combined forces earlier in an effort to stave off that possibility, lending their support when necessary to a nonpartisan ticket. In so doing, they secured the

---

[9]*Ibid.*, 206.
[10]Swisher, 32.

nomination of 32 favored at-large delegates from the state's four congressional districts.[11]

Now it was the turn of the Workingmen. Trying to dispel the impression that they were irresponsible radicals, they courted the farmers by claiming an identity of interest.[12] But the farmers were unable to agree upon leaders, and their hesitation allowed the nonpartisan alignment to enhance its political strength at the convention and in the subsequent voting. This was precisely the body of opinion that the young University of California would rely upon for friends. Thanks to the election of their candidate, the San Francisco attorney, Joseph Hoge, as president of the convention, the nonpartisan group was able to take effective control of the critical committee on education. The selection of Workingmen's delegate Jacob Freud of San Francisco (the youngest member of the convention) also improved the situation, for although he was a Workingmen's representative, ostensibly aligned with the University's detractors, he was also the only alumnus of the University present (Class of 1876). He proved to be an articulate and enthusiastic supporter of his alma mater. Another Workingmen's delegate on the committee whose natural sympathy lay with the University, was Eli Blackmer, a sometime superintendent of schools.

THE UNIVERSITY AND THE CONVENTION

Even though many convention delegates appeared favorable to the University cause, the situation was still uncertain in 1878. As opening day, September 28, approached, "every settled institution, the university included, trembled with fear of menaced calamities."[13] The threats for the University took two forms. Neither is new, given the long existence of universities, but one in particular is of especial importance in the history of American public universities. The first was a characteristic nineteenth-century view of a university education as "useful" or "practical," or as we might say today, "relevant." While these are not precise words—what is

---

[11]*The Argonaut*, April 20, 1878, 8. In San Francisco, the Workingmen won a major victory as the old parties could not overcome their self-interests and nominated rival slates.

[12]*Debates and Proceedings*, 18.

[13]William Carey Jones, *Illustrated History of the University of California* (San Francisco, 1895), 128.

practical in one situation is hardly so in another they do seem to imply a vocational or directly serviceable mission. Since education that appears to be "impractical" is often associated with wealthy and leisured elites, the debate over utility in the curriculum is often also a dispute between social groups over influence in the university and its curricula. The debate in the convention sometimes reflected this clash of social groups, often the Workingmen and farmers against the upper class associated with the regents.

The second threat facing the University's status quo is alive again in the 1990s: dissatisfaction with the process for selecting university boards of trustees, either because the members are viewed by some to be narrowly recruited or because it is alleged that they owe their appointments to favoritism, wealth, and political interest. Such criticisms of the regental selection process had emerged at nearly every session of the legislature during the University's first decade. The regents were understandably made nervous, especially by the populism of the Kearneyites and Kearney's own picture of armed Workingmen rising up against the rich or ringing the state capitol with bayonets. Even discounting the rhetorical exaggerations of his remarks, radicalism seemed to appeal to many citizens. *The Argonaut*, an antiradical paper, noted in an editorial that "[The calling of the Convention] was an opportunity for an outburst of all the devilish incendiarism with which the worst element of Democracy was charged. The pent-up fires of discontent, lawlessness, and crime burst forth."[14]

From letters written at the time of the convention, it is clear that those closely involved with the University were worried, if not outright pessimistic, about its ultimate fate. In March of 1878, John Dwinelle, author of the University's charter and one of its long-time supporters (and after whom a Berkeley campus building is named), discussed the situation with Daniel Coit Gilman, president from 1872 to 1875, and now president of Johns Hopkins. Replying to an apparently gloomy letter from Dwinelle regarding the forthcoming convention, Gilman was more optimistic: "I do not fully respond to your apprehensions that the bad forces sectarian and secular will overcome the good forces in control of the institution."[15] On the contrary, he was hopeful that the convention would in fact remedy the weaknesses

---

[14]*The Argonaut* (July 27, 1878), 8.
[15]Letter from D. C. Gilman to John W. Dwinelle dated March 20, 1878. *J. W. Dwinelle Papers,* Bancroft Library, University of California, Berkeley.

Figure 10: John W. Dwinelle, regent 1868-1874.

that existed in the University's internal organization.[16] However, Dwinelle, a San Francisco lawyer, authority on the judiciary, political journalist, and great friend of the University, who, in Gilman's words, had watched over the institution's early years as regent and member of the legislature with "a fraternal affection," was hardly reassured.

Further evidence of anxiety on the part of those close to the administration of the University can be found in a letter written shortly after the start of proceedings by Professor Martin Kellogg to Regent Winans, chair of the convention's committee on education. Kellogg had been intimately involved with the University from its inception and was, in 1878, dean of the Academic Senate and second ranking administrator. In his letter Kellogg suggested that, "Perhaps the friends of the university will wish to let the whole matter alone for fear of getting something worse rather than better,"[17] but he knew that in the previous session of the legislature a proposal providing for the election of regents from each of the state's congressional districts had been defeated. He certainly sensed that a fight was brewing and suggested that the regents be prepared with a plan because, "If only radical changes are proposed with no competing plans, then the case might go by default."[18]

Kellogg's letter of October 21, 1878, suggesting that it might be wise to avoid the question of what should go into the constitution concerning the University did not reach Sacramento until after Winans, on October 9, had proposed an entirely new article on education. Nonetheless, Winans seemed to have been in agreement with Kellogg's suggestion, for his proposed section on the University avoided the two controversial questions of legislative control and "practical" agricultural and mechanical instruction. Instead, his strategy was to concentrate on the matter of securing the Uni-

---

[16]Dwinelle must have assumed that legislation calling for the election of delegates would pass because Gilman's letter was written before the convention's enabling act became law.

[17]Letter from Martin Kellogg to J. W. Winans (October 21, 1878). *Correspondence and Papers of the Regents of the University of California, 1878-80*. University of California, Berkeley Archives, 2-3.

[18]*Ibid.*

Figure 11: Martin Kellogg, dean of the Academic Senate, 1870-1884.

versity's financial future by requiring income from the lands granted to the institution to "remain a permanent fund."[19]

It seems likely that Winans concurred with the opinion that no matter how strongly the regents wished to place favorable language into the constitution, discretion suggested that the potential dangers made the risks great and that caution and tact were needed. Unfortunately, Winans' hopes of avoiding the potentially explosive twin issues of legislative control and "practical education" were dashed when William F. White, a Workingmen's delegate from the Pajaro Valley, openly raised these matters before they could be sidetracked. He proposed that the curriculum was to be restructured in favor of utilitarian subjects, and until this was achieved, no state money was to be released to support the campus.[20]

Given his position as a member of the Board of Regents smarting under accusations of impropriety, Winans was in an awkward position, but other supporters of the University now came into the open, notably Walter Van Dyke. Van Dyke was a nonpartisan from Alameda County where the University was situated, and he had nominated Regent J. West Martin to fill the vacancy in the Alameda County delegation caused by the death of former governor and regents' legal counselor, Henry Haight. On October 22 Van Dyke defended the existing structure of University governance by introducing wording intended to demonstrate that the University's origin and subsequent development made it necessary that the institution's "organization and government . . . be perpetually continued in their existing form, character and condition."[21] He went on to propose that in the future the regents were to retain all the authority and rights currently enjoyed.

---

[19]*Debates and Proceedings*, 85. The University had received funds from the sale of lands granted to it by the Seminary of Learning Act of 1853, and from the sale of salt and marshlands, from the sale of land in Oakland, and most notably, by the Morrill Act of 1862. Throughout the 1870s, the Grangers and others had called for the separation of Morrill Act income from these other funds, and its exclusive use for the teaching of agriculture and the mechanic arts. Winans desired to keep the funds together to meet the University's overall needs. During the early years, the regents were concerned about the security of the institution's endowments. This was undoubtably on Winan's mind when he proposed his new section of the constitution. See also Verne Stadtman, *The University of California, 1868-1968* (New York, 1970), 111.

[20]*Ibid.*

[21]*Ibid.*, 172.

It was time for critics to raise the second issue. J. V. Webster, also of Alameda County, a farmer and a man who was to play a decisive role in the debate over the University, now offered the feared but expected motion that henceforth a majority of the regents were to be selected by popular vote (some *ex officio* regents were already in that category, if indirectly): "The University of this State shall be under the control of a Board of Regents, composed of fifteen members, two of which shall be elected from each Congressional District . . . for such a time as the Legislature may, by law, provide. The remaining seven shall be *ex officio* members."[22] (This motion was similar to bills that had been defeated in several sessions of the legislature prior to the calling of the convention.) No vote was taken on the motion.

THE REPORT OF THE COMMITTEE ON
EDUCATION AND DEBATE, JANUARY 20-22

On Monday, January 20, 1879, the 115th day of the convention, the Committee of the Whole commenced discussion of the report of its committee on education. Each of the 10 sections was separately scheduled for debate and voting, the section on the University was last. Winans put a good face on his committee's deliberations. "Your Committee, sir," he announced to the Committee of the Whole, "although . . . late in presenting their report, gave the subject their most patient investigation. They sat night after night in close deliberation, characterized by a harmony of feeling and a propriety of action, until they had discussed the whole question, and examined it in all its bearings."[23]

Why the report was "late," Winans did not say, and the committee apparently did not publish any minutes of its meetings.[24] Doubtless deeply held educational and philosophical principles made compromise unlikely, or acceptable wording was not readily forthcoming. But another explanation for a tardy report was that the education committee probably anticipated the

---

[22]*Ibid.*, 173. Webster's amendment was referred to the Committee on State Institutions and Public Buildings rather than to the Committee on Education.

[23]*Ibid.*, 1087.

[24]The material on the convention in the state archives in Sacramento is rather limited.

Figure 12: "Residence of J. V. Webster, Fruit Vale, Alameda, Co." from the *New Historical Atlas of Alameda County*, 1878.

divisions existing in the main body and thereby found agreeing even more difficult.

The ensuing debate in the Committee of the Whole was acrimonious. One delegate summed up the differences in this way: "One idea is that no portion of the public funds of this State should be appropriated to the education of the people of the State beyond a certain point," but the other idea was that "there is little danger of educating the people of the State too much."[25] These two philosophies, the one seeking to limit sharply the extent to which public education would be provided, and the other trying to make education more available, appeared throughout the discussions on the education committee's report. This was particularly true during the debate on the public school system, where delegates argued about whether foreign languages should be taught in the schools at public expense.

Another issue surfacing early—one related to the question of the process used to select regents—was central control over education on all levels, from primary through university. This was expressed in a number of distinct yet connected ways. First was the debate over payment of a superintendent of public instruction and his staff—hostility to high salaries was voiced.[26] Another issue was the elimination of a recommendation (Section 7) for a state board of education. Delegates evidently believed that money could be saved and local control of education maximized if decision making was concentrated at the county level. A third issue was the fear that centralized control would effectively hamstring local opinion regarding the selection of textbooks and the administration of teacher examinations. The low regard in which the legislature, and lobbyists who influenced it, were held, was very apparent in the remarks of a number of the delegates. As with so many other matters discussed by the delegates, methods to limit the authority over education of corruptible legislators over education were widely sought. Local control was seen by many to be a preferable option. As a matter of fact, however, this continuing sense of displeasure with Sacramento actually worked to the advantage of the University.

---

[25]*Debates and Proceedings*, 1087.
[26]*Ibid.*, 1093.

SECTION 10 ON THE UNIVERSITY AND THE
COMMITTEE OF THE WHOLE

In the afternoon session of the following day (January 21), the proposal on the University from the committee on education was read to the delegates. Section 10 provided that,

The University of California shall constitute a public trust, and its organization and government shall be perpetually continued in their existing form and character, subject only to such legislative control as may be necessary to insure compliance with the terms of its endowments, and of the several Acts of the Legislature of this State, and of the Congress of the United States, donating lands or money for its support. It shall be entirely independent from all political or sectarian influences, and kept free therefrom in the appointment of its Regents, and in the administration of its affairs.[27]

Immediately upon presentation of this general and unexceptional proposal two objections were raised. The first was an amendment offered by Volney Howard of Los Angeles calling for instruction in, "agriculture, mechanic arts, mineralogy, and the applied sciences."[28]

This familiar issue of useful learning was also implicit in the motion then introduced by J. V. Webster (who had earlier proposed a partially elected Board of Regents).[29] The second Webster proposal specified that funds received from the Land Grant or Morrill Act of 1862 should be separated from general University funds, the interest to be applied to the sole benefit of the colleges of agriculture and the mechanic arts. While ruled out of order on parliamentary grounds, Webster's amendment nevertheless focused debate. It also caused real concern among University supporters.

Webster, a past master of the State Grange, had long been active in agricultural organizations. His views consequently carried considerable political significance in a convention where so many delegates were either farmers or representatives of farming regions. Furthermore, the Webster amendment had the support of Workingmen delegates who had agreed to it at a caucus the night before the committee's report was presented to the

---

[27]*Ibid.*, 1109.
[28]*Ibid.*
[29]*Ibid.*, 1109-10.

Committee of the Whole.[30] The *Bulletin* reported that, "The country delegates to the number of thirty-five caucused on university topics last night [January 20, 1879], Superintendent Ezra Carr [State superintendent of public instruction and dismissed former University of California professor of agriculture] attended and explained the college endowments."[31] The caucus concluded that the kind of college of agriculture as envisioned by the Morrill Act did not exist at the University of California; they agreed to oppose the proposal of the committee on education and to support a new section to conform with their view of the aims of the Morrill Act.

Here was the alliance that University supporters had long feared. A view of the University was being proposed contrary to its historical evolution. It would be a university whose fundamental direction could be informed by narrow sectarian or economic interests—interests that regarded the curriculum as their special right or province and appropriated to its support the important sums of money released to the states by the national Morrill Act. Furthermore, the University's capacity to serve wider needs and to cooperate in defining those needs was also at stake, for the withdrawal of land grant money meant that subjects other than agriculture, mining, or mechanic arts would have to be supported separately.

On January 22, as the debate continued, W. W. Moreland, a lawyer and nonpartisan from Sonoma County, put forward the Grange's point of view: the very title of the Morrill Act—"an act donating public lands . . . [to] provide colleges for the benefit of agriculture and mechanic arts"[32]—proved its fundamental purpose, and anything else was a misappropriation of public money. Moreland ended his remarks by reading into the record a long article reprinted that morning in the *Sacramento Record-Union* from the *Western Homestead*, a publication from Kansas, another farming state. It began,

If Congress should appropriate half a million dollars to each State for the maintenance of a plow factory, and the Legislatures should use the money for the manufacture of astronomical telescopes or gilt-edged Hebrew dictionaries, people generally would indulge a faint suspicion that the Congressional appropriation had been grossly perverted . . . and [the University] now seeks, by a clause

---

[30]*San Francisco Evening Bulletin* (January 22, 1879), 1; and *The Sacramento Bee* (January 21, 1879), 3.
[31]*San Francisco Evening Bulletin* (January 21, 1879), 1.
[32]*Debates and Proceedings*, 1113.

in the new Constitution of that State to forever secure to itself the million or more granted by Congress to an "Agricultural College," and which million or more it gobbled several years since, despite the protest of the farmers and mechanics of that State.[33]

But historical arguments, particularly at critical moments, are rarely a simple question of polarities. The dispute over the future disposition of Morrill Land Grant monies in California was also part of a different and in some respects larger issue of public land management in the state. The University's stewardship of the land granted by the Morrill Act became an issue at the convention on January 22, 1879, when it was reported that the institution had sold more than its allocated acreage. Two bills pending in Congress confused the delegates still more. One bill gave the University the opportunity to return some of the worthless land it had selected and to replace it with other and potentially valuable land. This was obviously a bill the regents would favor. The other bill, however, was supported by an alleged land schemer and appeared to have the purpose of allowing "land sharks" to swindle settlers out of their homes.

While the regents disclaimed any affiliation with legislation concealing private under the guise of public interests, Workingmen delegates remained suspicious that the regents were intent on land grabbing, especially as several former members of the board had acquired huge holdings during the preceding three decades. "If the university cannot be perpetuated without entailing misery, by oppression and by injustice," said San Francisco's Workingmen's delegate Charles Beerstecher, "if it can only rise amid the tears and groans of outraged families, then . . . it had better sink to the ground."[34]

While the Workingmen delegates supported the farmers in their criticism of the Committee on Education's report and the existing College of Agriculture, the former were more concerned with the issue of popular control over governmental bodies such as the regents. N. G. Wyatt of Monterey County, openly disapproved of the committee's proposal and argued that he did not want to "canonize [the University] as being the perfection of wisdom and goodness, and crystallize it into a monument that could never be changed."[35] Beerstecher added, "Why should there not be a

---

[33]*Ibid.*, 1114.
[34]*Ibid.*, 1355.
[35]*Ibid.*, 1114.

power to change its form, and to change its character?"[36] The criticism came to a climax in a statement by Henry Larkin, Workingmen's candidate for convention president, when he said: "In our State, provision is made for a change of the Constitution, but this remarkable section provides that this institution, created by law shall not be changed."[37]

UNIVERSITY OPPOSITION TO WEBSTER'S PROPOSED AMENDMENT

Opposition to the interpretation of the Morrill Act offered by Webster and Moreland came quickly from the regents and their friends. They held that the language of the act of 1862 made it clear that more than instruction in agriculture and the mechanic arts was intended by Congress. The scientific and classical could not be excluded. Regent Winans told the delegates that the Morrill Act was "the statement of a comprehensive scheme for promoting the higher education of the people,"[38] and the colleges founded from the act were to be infinitely more than agricultural colleges.

Several delegates strongly argued that the separation of the Morrill Act funds from other University funds as required by the Webster amendment was a violation of the contract made by California with the federal government when the land granted to the state in 1862 was accepted.[39] Citing provisions in the Supreme Court's Dartmouth College case of 1819 as a precedent, these delegates claimed that accepting Webster's narrow interpretation of the Morrill Act's provisions would result in California's forfeiture of federal land grant money. A broader interpretation of the Morrill Act would include agriculture as part of the legitimate studies of a university and its conception of knowledge. Agriculture in this view was a science as much as a "mechanical art."

The influence of Daniel Coit Gilman on those who defended the regents' interpretation of the Morrill Land Grant Act was much in evidence. His philosophy still guided the "inclusionists," regents such as Winans, Hager, and Martin, who defended the integration of the college of agriculture into the University of California. Gilman had maintained that this was

---

[36]*Ibid.*, 1116.
[37]*Ibid.*, 1119.
[38]*Ibid.*, 1111.
[39]*Ibid.*, 1117, 1121.

no less than Senator Morrill's conception of the nature of a land grant university: Gilman, while still at Yale, had had the senator as a house guest and thus had had "what amounted to a private seminar on [his] intentions in introducing the [Land Grant Act of 1862]."[40] During the debate on January 21, Winans read a lengthy report from Gilman into the record of the convention.[41] It outlined the work of the University's college of agriculture under its newly appointed professor, Eugene W. Hilgard, and attempted to show that the University was faithful to the intentions of those who had established it in 1868 following the grant of federal land six years earlier.

Debate concerning the University did not follow any pattern. Delegates, whether detractors or supporters, jumped from topic to topic without any observable plan. More than one measure lay unenacted on the floor. This behavior was typical of the proceedings from the beginning. According to *The Sacramento Bee,* the convention lacked overall floor leadership.[42] President Hoge could not hold the delegates to any semblance of parliamentary order; many of them were neophytes, lacking any knowledge of or sympathy with the practices and niceties of legislative behavior. Strategies, counter-strategies, and amendments haphazardly followed. Furthermore, the delegates were obviously confused about how to guarantee the University's accountability, whether it should be to the state or the public, or whether the legislature ought to play a more central and direct role in the University's governance. The press remarked that "the State University nut appears a hard one for the convention to crack."[43]

Finally, a substitute amendment that appeared to be consistent with the aims and hopes of the University's supporters, was put to a Committee of the Whole and passed by a vote of 68 to 49. The amendment was made by Thomas Laine of Santa Clara, who, fearing that the University might be placed in "bands of iron" and constrained in its growth, stressed the need for popular support of the state's university. His amendment declared the University of California,

> to be a perpetual institution of this State, organized to administer
> a great public trust, and the Legislature shall have no power to
> impair or divert any gift, grant, or donation made to it, from the

---

[40]Stadtman, *University of California,* 62.

[41]*Debates and Proceedings,* 1110-12.

[42]*The Sacramento Bee* (December 18, 1878), 2.

[43]*The Sacramento Bee* (January 22, 1879), 3.

purposes or objects of those making such gift, grant, or donation; its officers shall hold office for such time as the Legislature may prescribe. Instructions [sic] shall be therein given, in addition to other matters, in agriculture, metallurgy, the mechanic arts and applied science; it shall be entirely independent of all political and sectarian influences.[44]

Although at the close of discussion on January 22, the University received this seemingly favorable endorsement, the crucial wording was the phrase "its officers shall hold office for such time as the legislature may prescribe." Despite the fact that Laine's resolution seemed to affirm the University's intentions, the offending phrase opened the door to precisely the kind of intervention University supporters had all along attempted to prevent; and despite the random nature of debate throughout the convention, the likelihood of failure on the part of opponents could not be taken for granted.

Nearly a month later, on February 18, the unfavorable Laine amendment came up for discussion before the convention. Webster once again intervened with a motion that was surprisingly far more attenuated than his two earlier ones. He now accepted the principle that the University of California "shall constitute a public trust . . . perpetually continued in the form and character prescribed by the Organic Act . . . subject only to such legislative control as may be necessary as to insure compliance with the terms of its endowments and the proper investment and security of its funds." He emphasized that it "shall be entirely independent of all political and sectarian influence, and kept free therefrom in the appointment of its Regents and in the administration of its affairs." He accepted the interpretation of the land grant university as a place where scientific and classical studies—as well as "military tactics"—would be taught. He added, however, an important proviso that,

all the moneys derived from the sale of the public lands donated to this State by Act of Congress, approved July 2, 1862, and the several Acts amendatory thereof, shall be invested as provided by said Act of Congress [the Morrill Act]; and the interest of said moneys shall be inviolably appropriated to the endowment, support, and maintenance of at least one college of agriculture, where the leading objects shall be . . . to teach such branches of

---

[44]*Debates and Proceedings*, 1123.

learning as are related to scientific and practical agriculture and the mechanic arts, in accordance with the requirements and conditions of said Act of Congress.[45]

This amendment, he said, "secures the permanency of the University and at the same time secures a proper distribution, and that the funds shall be appropriated for the purposes for which they are donated."[46]

While there was some similarity between this and the amendments Webster had introduced on January 21 and February 18, important differences need to be stressed. The earlier proposals had said nothing about permanently maintaining the organization and government of the University in their original form. Furthermore, Webster's initial motion had been quite specific in requiring Morrill Act revenue to be used exclusively for colleges teaching agriculture and mechanic arts. But this last motion was far less restrictive. Essentially, it restated the language of the Morrill Act of 1862 with all its vagueness and imprecision. An obvious shift in Webster's thinking had taken place, and his February proposal was much more compatible with the measure originally entertained by the majority on the Committee on Education.

Nevertheless, Webster's motion failed to carry—possibly as much because of the restiveness of the delegates and the confusion over amendments, as because of the precise wording of his text and its meaning. That this may be the correct interpretation for what happened seems justified by events occurring just eight days later when Webster once again offered his amendment, this time during a second reading of the article on education. Now, however, the amendment received the support of no less a person than Regent Winans who used it to attack Laine's proposal as "the very worst of all those which have been presented to this body" because it threw the University "into the hands of the legislature." Winans went on to present the regents' case for the stability of institutions, essential to the University's survival, growth, and prosperity:

Now, in all these great institutions it is a cardinal principle that they must be stable. They must be beyond all power of assault and subversion, or they will be a failure. There are men in this State who are anxious to make donations to this institution the moment it is placed upon a permanent basis. But so long as it is made

---

[45]*Ibid.*, 1401.
[46]*Ibid.*

subject to legislative caprice; so long as it can be made subject to the beck of politicians; so long as it can be made to subserve sectarian or political designs, it never will flourish. . . . It was urged that if it is made permanent, then the Legislature would have no control. Not so. This present system was adopted ten years ago, and has not only had a magical effect, but has developed the noblest college existing on the continent. This amendment now pending meets the wishes of the Regents and of that class of agriculturists who take an interest in this institution. I hope gentlemen will stand by to repel all unfriendly assaults upon the University of California.[47]

Soon after, the delegates voted on the Webster substitute motion, passing it by a vote of 70-59, and it thereby became the approved Section 9 (formerly Section 10) of the article on education.[48]

The entire article on education subsequently was affirmed by a vote of 86-45. In other sections of the article relating to the public schools, the delegates voted to provide state support only to common, that is, elementary schools, thus rendering a serious blow to the high school movement and jeopardizing college enrollments that required a strong system of secondary feeder schools. The examination of teachers and the selection of textbooks were thrown back on school districts to assure local control and prevent the potential corruptive influences of the legislature.

Several days later, on March 3, the delegates approved the new state constitution by a vote of 120-15, and the convention, having completed its business, adjourned *sine die*. Adoption of the constitution came before the voters of California on May 17, 1879, and passed.

REASONS FOR THE PASSAGE OF SECTION 9 ON THE UNIVERSITY

The Webster amendment adopted on February 18 established the University's independence and declared the institution to be a "public trust." Section 9 reaffirmed: (1) the regents were eligible for 16-year terms thus

---

[47]*Ibid.*, 1476, emphasis mine.

[48]Section 10 of the Article on Education became Section 9 when the proposed section concerning and State Board of Education was eliminated on January 21, 1879.

minimizing the appointive power of any single governor. As a "public trust" the university regents were not state officers whose terms were limited to four years; (2) the legislature could not alter the University's organization and government from the patterns laid down in the Organic Act; and (3) political influence was to be excluded from the conduct of the University's affairs. These three provisions must be viewed as major victories for Regent Winans and his colleagues who had fought hard to prevent drastic changes in the University's government. They had achieved several important goals. Yet, it is necessary to look further at the language contained in the Webster amendment.

While making allowance for the maintenance of the concept of a public trust and the permanence of the University's existing structure free from political interference, the Webster amendment made these provisions contingent upon the proper investment of the funds derived from the Morrill Act. Webster's words indicated that the University would have the safeguards it desired "provided" that certain conditions were met. The first part of the amendment was conditional upon the second part. In short, the Webster amendment appears to have been a compromise agreement.

Who exactly were the parties to the compromise and what was its nature? How had the alliances and groupings described at the opening of the convention by Henry George fared in the interim? The final debate that led to the approval of the amendment provides a clue as to the meaning of the negotiations. In proposing his amendment, Webster had said, "It is at the earnest request of the friends of the University that I offer it now."[49] Winans then supported the amendment by saying that it "meets the wishes of the Regents, and of that class of agriculturists who take an interest in this Institution."[50] Of the two statements, that of Winans is the more significant because it clearly shows the support of both the regents and a segment of the farmers. While undoubtedly trying to win additional farmers to his side, his remarks suggest that there were significant differences of opinion among the agriculturists that the University's defenders could possibly exploit, and some farmers appear to have been won over to the side of the regents and their new ally, J. V. Webster.

Webster and Winans might appear to have been unlikely collaborators in a joint venture. Time and time again Winans argued for the independence

---

[49]*Debates and Proceedings*, 1476.
[50]*Ibid.*

of the University and defended it against the accusations of its critics, farmers amongst them.   On the other hand, Webster had at one time introduced a proposal to restructure the Board of Regents as a partly elected body. The regents had fought similar proposals throughout much of the 1870s and twice defeated them in the legislature.   Later, in the convention, Webster had tried to separate the general University Fund from the revenue derived from the Morrill Act land sales, in support of the colleges of agriculture and mechanic arts.

Webster's amendments to alter the selection of regents and to modify its funding practices had become the focus of much of the debate about the University.   He had been openly criticized for his efforts to modify the University, an institution which, as one delegate reminded him, was located in his home county of Alameda.   The *Oakland Tribune*, a paper that strongly backed the University, had censured him.[51]   Subsequently, in debate with Regent Hager, Webster had raised the issue of the Political Code's requirement for the students to do physical work in the fields and gardens of the agricultural college.   On all of these occasions, he hardly seemed a likely candidate to announce to the convention that "It is at the earnest request of the friends of the University that I offer it now."[52]

The Webster amendment carried by only 11 votes. Analysis of the balloting reveals that the amendment received its support primarily from the nonpartisans, that many of the lawyers in the convention backed it, and that a group of farmers or representatives of farming areas also gave it their votes. The importance of the representatives of farming cannot be overemphasized.   Of the 152 delegates, 87 came from agricultural areas.   It has been asserted that the agricultural counties had the political power to control the convention if their delegates voted appropriately.   But, on the Webster amendment the farmers actually split, with half voting in favor, the other half against.

A majority of the Workingmen from San Francisco and the mining areas voted against the amendment, although by then, late in the convention, the Workingmen's once solid ranks had been broken, and they no longer voted as a unit. Indeed, 13 Workingmen voted for the Webster amendment.

---

[51]*Oakland Evening Tribune* (December 27 and 28, 1878).   University of California, Berkeley, Archives Scrapbook #1, p. 209.

[52]*Debates and Proceedings*, 1476.

The salient fact all along was that none of Henry George's three blocs had the voting strength to succeed alone. Therefore, each bloc had to obtain additional support from one or both of the other two voting blocs while holding on to as much of its own group as possible. This process was evident during the voting on the Webster amendment.

The importance of the representatives of farming cannot be overemphasized. Of the 152 delegates, 87 came from agricultural areas. It has been asserted that the agricultural counties had the political power to control the convention if their delegates voted appropriately.[53]

While the University of California emerged from the convention stronger and more secure politically than before, other sectors of education did not fare, as we have seen, quite so well. How can we account for the University's singularly good fortune? Why did potentially hostile delegates from farming areas and many Workingmen vote with the regents to pass the Webster amendment at the convention's eleventh hour?

REASONS FOR THE UNIVERSITY'S SUCCESS

At least four reasons can be provided: (1) control of the convention by sentiment favorable to the University; (2) the influence of Regent Winans; (3) a general dissatisfaction with legislative control; and (4) the importance of agriculture and the University's special cultivation of the farming interest.

The election of Joseph Hoge as president of the Constitutional Convention marked the beginning of a significant series of events. In the days that followed, the nonpartisans selected most of the convention's officers and filled the vacancies in the ranks of delegates unable to serve. They dominated the appointments to more than 30 committees. It was to these committees that the multitude of proposed sections of the constitution were referred, and from which was reported the legislation debated on the floor. Since the committees had an opportunity to discuss at considerable length the matters sent to them, their reports had to be taken seriously. That a proposed section to the constitution was referred out to the Committee of the Whole gave it a certain legitimacy. Other proposals died in committee

---

[53]Moorehead, 292. Moorehead claimed that, "the changes made in the organic law by the convention were inaugurated and sanctioned by the representatives of the agricultural sections of the State." And that, "all the chief grievances held by the farmers against the old constitution were remedied by the new one."

and never came before the convention. Thus, the makeup of the committees was crucial.

Repeatedly, Regent Winans spoke in defense of the University and the report of the Committee on Education. His role as chairman provided him with an opportunity to introduce, explain, and defend each section of the education article. Early in the consideration of the section on the University, he gave a long speech in which he described the development of the College of Agriculture, explained the Morrill Act, outlined the organization of the regents, reported on the financial condition of the University, and recounted aspects of its educational philosophy.[54] His lengthy oration served to educate the delegates on a number of important issues; in another instance, he patiently explained why the term "public trust" had been used: to allow the regents to have terms of 16 years.[55]

At other times Winans acted as parliamentary strategist. He knew when and how to incorporate wording that appeared unfavorable to the University but could actually strengthen its appeal, as when he supported Howard's amendment calling for the University to "provide for instruction in agriculture, mechanic arts, mineralogy, and the applied sciences."[56] Stating that the University was already doing this, Winans also saw the psychological advantage of incorporating these words into the committee's report. By adding a few words with no real significance, he hoped to win additional votes. At still other times, he proved to be a skillful and lively debater, promptly responding to claims that students in the college of agriculture were being drawn toward the more traditional branches of learning, and successfully defending the regents against charges of mismanagement.

Winans' work did not go unrecognized. After his death one newspaper said of him that he "adhered to the original purpose of placing the university beyond the domain of politics. . . . The end he sought was attained and the article of the Constitution of California regarding the university represents in large measure [his] work."[57] The Bar Association of San Francisco declared that "largely to his instrumentality the State University was placed

---

[54]*Debates and Proceedings*, 1110-12.
[55]*Ibid.*, 1119.
[56]*Ibid.*, 1109.
[57]*San Francisco Evening Bulletin* (March 31, 1887), 2.

securely beyond the realm of political control."[58] And the Board of Regents concluded that "mainly due to Mr. Winans' endeavor, we have the present clause in our State Constitution relating to the university."[59] The regents' memorial noted both his public and behind-the-scenes accomplishments, "the influence of his speeches," and his "persuasion in private."[60]

As we have seen, criticisms of an appointed Board of Regents were not lacking, and young Jacob Freud, the Workingmen's intellectual representative, could be counted among the critics. The regents appeared to fit Dennis Kearney's definition of the "rich who have ruled us until they have ruined us." The article from the *Western Homestead* read into the record by Moreland had described the regents as "a close corporation, filling all vacancies."[61] J. V. Webster, while not a Workingmen's delegate, had earlier proposed the compromise solution of a partially elected board, and others argued that a popularly elected body would direct the University curriculum along more practical lines.

When the final vote on the University was taken, however, Freud, Moreland, and Webster reversed themselves. Others also broke with what might have been expected to have been an antiregent position in sustaining the final Webster amendment. Their actions appear puzzling, but in context their votes are understandable and logical. On the one hand, they feared appointed officials as representatives of the classes that had stymied reform and had profited at a time when others faced hard circumstances. On the other hand, alternative arrangements—an elected board of regents, or one responsible to an elected legislature—began to seem no better and even worse. Freud, in explaining his changed position, reasoned:

> No person more sincerely objects to the appointment of public officers than I, whenever it can be avoided with policy and wisdom, but sir, experience has invariably shown that the election of Regents involves the destruction and ruin of the University.

---

[58] *In Memoriam, Joseph Webb Winans*, a statement of the Bar Association of San Francisco; Bancroft Library, University of California, Berkeley; emphasis mine.

[59] "Memorial to the Late Regent Winans," Annual Report of the Secretary to the Board of Regents of the University of California for the Year Ending June 30, 1887, (State Office, Sacramento, 1887), 7. Emphasis mine.

[60] *Ibid.* "Persuasion in private" is difficult for the historian to verify.

[61] *Debates and Proceedings*, 1114.

Political prejudices and conspiracies creep into the institution and poison its best blood and vitiate its highest energies.[62]

The regents effectively exploited this sentiment, appealing to the underlying disrespect for California's legislature. Hager for one asked the delegates,

How many of you learned men could better administer that trust than it has been administered? Look at the administration of public affairs in the State, city, county, and municipal governments. See how they have been administered, and compare it with the administration of this fund belonging to the University and the State of California.[63]

Martin and Winans had staked their reputations on their denials of misconduct. It is likely that the opinion and reputations of these men influenced the more reasonable among their political opponents.

For example, Delegate Shafter summed up one reaction to charges of regental self-interest by stating, "Why do not these gentlemen [critics] specify in what they [the regents] have been dishonest? If they have stolen anything, why do not these persons indicate where and when?"[64] Would it not be better to entrust the University to these respected civic leaders, known to be honorable men, for 16-year terms, which allowed for continuity and planning, than to the uncertainties of the elective process and the instability of high turnovers?

It is clear that the regents were extremely eager to replace the language that the convention had adopted some weeks earlier—the Laine amendment that specified legislative control and that Winans had called "the very worst of all those which have been presented to this body."[65] Furthermore, the convention was heading into its final days. The available time for action was disappearing. Thus, the motivation for the regents to accept, and, indeed, to seek out a compromise was real. For university supporters and for Winans, in particular, securing solid foundations for the institution was the preeminent concern. No university could thrive under conditions of

---

[62]*Ibid.*, 1110.
[63]*Ibid.*, 1118.
[64]*Ibid.*, 1120.
[65]*Ibid.*, 1476.

insecurity. Winans said: "in all these great institutions it is a cardinal principle that they must be stable."[66]

Distrust of the legislature and fears that the state would not protect rural interests led the Grange members into compromising, but this does not mean that they lost sight of their objectives and simply bowed to circumstances. The meaning of their compromise still needs to be stressed and explained; for not only did they possess the votes necessary to accomplish their legislative goals, they actually did put this political power to work to gain their objectives in the convention. Throughout the 1870s, farming leaders, often associated with the Granger movement, had criticized the University's efforts in agricultural education and advocated the separation of the agricultural and mechanic arts colleges from the University. They were not likely to be satisfied with the Webster compromise unless it granted them positive advantages. The *San Francisco Evening Bulletin* observed that the "friends of the university came forward with a substitute [the revised Webster amendment] which was acceptable to the sense of the country delegates and thus won an easy victory."[67]

We have consequently arrived at a point in the story where we can better understand Webster's seemingly disingenuous statement that he was reintroducing his proposal "at the earnest request of the friends of the university" and Winans' assertion that the Webster amendment had the support of "that class of agriculturists who take an interest in the institution."

While the grounds for compromise are rather clear in the case of the regents, the basis for the farmers' action is less obvious, their reasons more subtle, and their goals more varied. The regents would get the stability they desired provided the University supported a flourishing college of agriculture. But what did the farmers really hope to gain from compromise? For one thing, they would succeed in having the basic language of the Morrill Act written into the California constitution, thereby firmly identifying the University of California with its land grant heritage in perpetuity. However else the revenues from the sale of the Morrill lands might be used, they would have to support, in the words of the Morrill Act, "at least one College of Agriculture, where the leading objects shall be, without excluding other scientific and classical studies and including military tactics, to teach such

---

[66]*Ibid.*
[67]*San Francisco Evening Bulletin* (February 27, 1879), 1.

branches of learning as are related to scientific and practical agriculture and the mechanic arts."

However, the mere insertion of this wording into the constitution would not in itself be of great practical value. As we can see, the Morrill Act language is ambiguous, and, since its passage in 1862, could be and was interpreted differently by political leaders, educators, and ordinary citizens. Certainly it was during the debates of the Constitutional Convention of 1878-79. Merely inserting Morrill Act wording into the California constitution did not guarantee the farmers' aims.

It must then be assumed that the farmers gained something even more tangible. William Carey Jones concluded that the Webster amendment "more fully [provided] for the observance of the terms of the Morrill Act of 1862."[68] The farmers' second and most important victory, therefore, was the promise of a more completely developed College of Agriculture within the University. We must now ask what did this entail and what was its significance?

The first professor of agriculture, Ezra Carr, was seen by University authorities as having done little for the farmers except conspire with some of the leaders of the Grangers against President Gilman and the regents. Carr was fired in 1874, and his successor as professor of agriculture was Eugene W. Hilgard. This appointment was one of the masterstrokes of Gilman's administration. Yet no newcomer ever inherited a more difficult situation. The rural press let him know that he was not universally welcome. Few students attended his classes, in part because of a boycott initiated by the Grangers.[69] In 1877, Hilgard had to report to the University president that, "No juniors or third-year students presented themselves for the agricultural courses during the past session. Consequently, there will be no senior students during the coming session, and therefore, no graduates of the College of Agriculture."[70] Undaunted, he put his efforts into demonstrating the importance of "scientific agriculture." Repeatedly he warned that the day would arrive when it would take more than scratching the ground to

---

[68] Jones, 130.

[69] E. W. Hilgard, "Some Reminiscences of Dr. Daniel C. Gilman," *University of California Chronicle*, XI, (January 1909), 24.

[70] *Report to the President of the University from the Colleges of Agriculture and the Mechanic Arts*, University of California, Berkeley (Sacramento: State Office, 1899), 4.

grow a successful crop in California. When that time came, the farmer would need to apply the scientific concepts that were beginning to be developed in laboratories like his.

Hilgard's work and his plans for the College of Agriculture were reported to the convention on January 21, 1879, when Winans read a lengthy report from Gilman. Obviously while some of the delegates knew Hilgard personally or knew of his reputation, the rest learned of him through this report. There is evidence that Hilgard's work had already had an effect upon a number of the farmers with whom he had contact. The story of his winning over a hostile group of farmers at a meeting shortly after his arrival in California and the statement of one of their leaders that, "By God, the man knows something," approaches legendary status.[71] A report issued in 1878 by an alumni group provides further evidence of his effectiveness:

> This department [agriculture] has in the past been grossly abused and misrepresented. Recently, however, the farmers of our state, individually and collectively as Grangers, have been informing themselves concerning our university's work in this department, and we think such as have learned the character of that work are invariably gratified at the result.[72]

Hilgard's scientific work was so extensive that it would have been difficult to believe that it did not have a positive effect upon at least some farmers. Soon after his arrival in Berkeley, Hilgard was advocating an agricultural survey of the state that would examine the various crops and soils that made up California's unique landscape. Berkeley quickly became an experiment station. Many agriculturists already were sending samples of soils, rocks, and crops to Hilgard for analysis, and he was able to report on methods to combat the alkali soils that plagued many farmers. He was also playing an important role in efforts to rejuvenate the wine industry in California. "I think," he said, "that the useful information thus obtained and spread over the state through the channels referred to, as well as some public meetings and discussions in which I have been enabled to participate, have

---

[71]The story as reported by Professor Wickson of the College of Agriculture at a memorial address upon Hilgard's death may be found in at least several sources, including Ferrier, *Origins*.

[72]Report of a Committee of the University Alumni Association on the University of California, 1878; in *Pamphlets Historical*, University of California, Berkeley, Archives.

Figure 13: Eugene Woldemar Hilgard, professor of agriculture, 1875-1905.

been instrumental in exciting a good deal of interest among farmers, and in promoting a better understanding of the aims and objectives of the agricultural department of the university."[73] Hilgard anticipated establishing local experiment stations in the various agricultural regions of the state. He hoped that the local Grangers and agricultural societies would cooperate in the work of such stations.[74]

Writing in 1877, he reflected that "With better means at my command, I would have accomplished much more than I have done during the past two years; and what I have now to show must serve mainly as a sample of the kind of work intended to be done hereafter." He then made his plea. "And I trust that in calling upon the coming legislature for some provision enabling us to place this department upon a more efficient footing, we shall have the support of the farmers' influence."[75] In a letter of the same year to George Davidson, the Head of the U.S. Coast and Geodetic Survey in California, he hoped "to obtain some more adequate provision from the incoming legislature, with the consent of even the Grangers."[76]

His efforts were rewarded with some success, for in his 1879 report he announced that the legislature had appropriated $5,000 a year for two years for the College of Agriculture. In his next two reports he asked for even larger appropriations, knowing that the state's agricultural progress and the development of his department were of considerable importance to the farmers and their elected representatives in the legislature. He had a good bargaining position and lost no opportunity to use it to advantage.

The farmers evidently believed, and apparently correctly, that their political pressure would force the regents to pay more attention to a College of Agriculture. The departure of Gilman for the East Coast had left the University without a strong president, and members of the Grange may have reasoned that the situation worked in their favor. There was a vacuum that a professor like Hilgard could fill; and, indeed, without his influence, the

---

[73]*Report to the President of the University from the Colleges of Agriculture and the Mechanic Arts. op. cit.*, 15-16.

[74]*Ibid.*, 13.

[75]*Ibid.*, 16.

[76]Letter from E. W. Hilgard to George Davidson (November 11, 1877), *George Davidson Papers*, University of California, Berkeley, Bancroft Library.

result in Sacramento would have been much different.[77] Hilgard's reputation for the work he had already accomplished in California and the promise of what he would achieve in the future won over enough farming votes to carry the Webster amendment, with its promise of political stability for the University.[78]

OTHER REASONS FOR SUPPORT OF SECTION 9

Any number of explanations can be offered to account for the passage of the Webster amendment. For example, there may have been a women's issue. Delegate James Ayers had moved to further amend the Webster amendment by adding, "No person shall be debarred admission to any of the collegiate department of the university on account of sex," and this carried on an overwhelming vote of 103-20. W. J. Tinnin, the Workingmen's delegate, later claimed that an alliance between the supporters of the University and advocates of women's suffrage accounted for the passage of the Webster amendment.[79] Yet this explanation does not entirely hold. For example, a delegate who earlier had appealed to the convention to consider having a woman sit on the board of regents ended up voting against the Webster amendment. Of course, the inevitable play of unforeseen circumstances certainly operated. Delegate Laine, excoriated by Regent Winans, apparently left for home before Webster, at the last hour, again introduced

---

[77]As E. J. Wickson, former dean, wrote in 1916, "A single significant token on his [Hilgard's] victory may be seen in the fact that within five years of his coming, the State Master [Delegate Webster] of the organization [the Grange] which set itself and its ten thousand members to the task of segregation of the College of Agriculture from the University presented, in the Constitutional Convention of 1879, the article which made the Organic Act of the University a part of the constitution of the state, and thus lifted the integrity of the institution above legislative dismemberment." ("Address by E. J. Wickson" in "Address at Memorial Services in Honor of Dr. E. W. Hilgard, University of California (January 30, 1916).") *University of California Chronicle*, XVIII (April 1916), 167.

[78]In the years that followed the convention, Hilgard continued to apply pressure to the University's General Fund in order to develop his college, and he succeeded. The College of Agriculture asked for and received larger appropriations from the state for its work. As Stadtman (p. 154) has stated, "Hilgard made the University's College of Agriculture a friend the farmer could not do without."

[79]*San Francisco Evening Bulletin* (March 13, 1879), 1.

his ultimately successful amendment.[80] Laine's absence and the rush of the delegates to end their lengthy stay in Sacramento may well have played a part in the acceptance of the Webster plan.

CONCLUSION

No explanations are wholly satisfying, but taken together the various accounts do provide a comprehensive picture of the social and political infighting in California in the period of the Second Constitutional Convention, and they are as close an approximation to the historical causes of the University's resurrection as a "fourth branch of government" as the evidence allows.

The success of the University's position was achieved by the practical control of the convention's organization by the nonpartisans and friends of Regent Winans, aided by the pervasive distrust of elected legislatures, and, through the reputation of Professor Hilgard, the University's successful cultivation of elements within the representatives of agricultural interests. But however accomplished, the outcome was favorable to the University in the long run. Throughout many other times of difficulty, the independence gained by the University of California in 1879 has served it and the people of the state effectively and well. That "independence" cannot be separated from questions of social sensitivity and public legitimacy. Nevertheless, within those parameters, the parameters of American democracy, independence has proven to be a leading factor in the University's ability to serve California's innumerable constituencies which today, as in 1879, often hold radically differing conceptions of the public good or the proper role of a state-assisted university.

---

[80]John A. Douglass, "Creating a Fourth Branch of Government: The University of California and the Constitutional Convention of 1879," *History of Education Quarterly*, 32 (Spring 1992): 61-62. Douglass believes that Laine's absence may have encouraged Webster to introduce his amendment again. Laine did return for the final days of the convention.

APPENDIX 1

The California Constitutional Convention, 1878-79
A Chronology of Events Relating to the University of California

1878

September 28   Convention opens.

September 30   Joseph Hoge elected president.

October 8   Committee on Education appointed by Hoge. Regent J. W. Winans chairman.

October 9   White's proposal to limit University instruction to that "of a practical nature," and prohibiting use of state funds for other purposes.

October 9   Winans' proposal to provide for a permanent University fund.

October 22   Van Dyke's proposal concerning the University.

October 22   Webster's proposal for a partially elected Board of Regents.

1879

January 20   Report of the Committee on Education, Sections 1 to 10 referred to the Committee of the Whole.

January 21   Committee on Education's proposal on the University, Section 10, before the Committee of the Whole.

January 21   Webster amendment to limit Morrill Act funds to support of the "Colleges of Agriculture and Mechanic Arts."

January 22   Webster amendment of January 21 defeated. Laine amendment adopted by the Committee of the Whole.

February 18   Section on the University (Laine amendment) before the convention.

February 18   Webster's revised proposal introduced and defeated.

February 26   Webster again offers the amendment defeated on February 18. Webster amendment adopted. Article on education approved.

March 3   Revised constitution approved by the convention.

March 3   Constitutional Convention adjourns.

May 17   Revised constitution approved by the voters

APPENDIX 2

Delegates and Other Persons who Played Important Roles in the Convention and in the History of the University of California

Ezra S. Carr	State Superintendent of Public Instruction. Dismissed first professor of agriculture at the University of California (1869-74). Active in the Granger movement.
John W. Dwinelle	As assemblyman from Alameda (not a delegate), introduced the University's Organic Act in 1868.
Jacob Freud	Workingmen's delegate from San Francisco. Only University of California alumnus in the convention. Member of the Committee on Education.
Daniel Coit Gilman	Second president of the University of California (1972-75) and founding president of the Johns Hopkins University.
Eugene W. Hilgard	Professor of Agriculture at the University of California (appointed in 1874).
Joseph Hoge	President of the convention, a nonpartisan delegate from the First Congressional District (San Francisco). Appointed delegates to committees and directed the convention's business.
Martin Kellogg	Dean of the Academic Senate, University of California.
Thomas Laine	Santa Clara County. Former member of the state legislature. Introduced amendment concerning the University which, until late in the convention, stood as the will of the body.

Justin S. Morrill — As a member of Congress introduced the Land Grant College Act of 1862.

Walter Van Dyke — Nonpartisan delegate from the Second Congressional District. On October 22, 1878, introduced section on the University.

Jonathan V. Webster — Nonpartisan delegate from Alameda County. Former grand master of the State Grange. Introduced unsuccessful amendments to establish a Board of Regents with a majority of elected members, and to restrict the use of income from the Morrill Land Grant to the colleges of agriculture and the mechanic arts. Introduced the amendment concerning the University of California that was adopted by the convention.

William F. White — Workingmen's delegate from Santa Cruz, Monterey, and San Benito Counties. Introduced amendment to require all University of California instruction to be of "a practical character" and restricted to agriculture and mechanic arts. Until this was done, no state money was to be expended for the University's support.

Joseph Webb Winans — Chairman of the Committee on Education, regent of the University of California. Nonpartisan delegate from the First Congressional District (San Francisco).